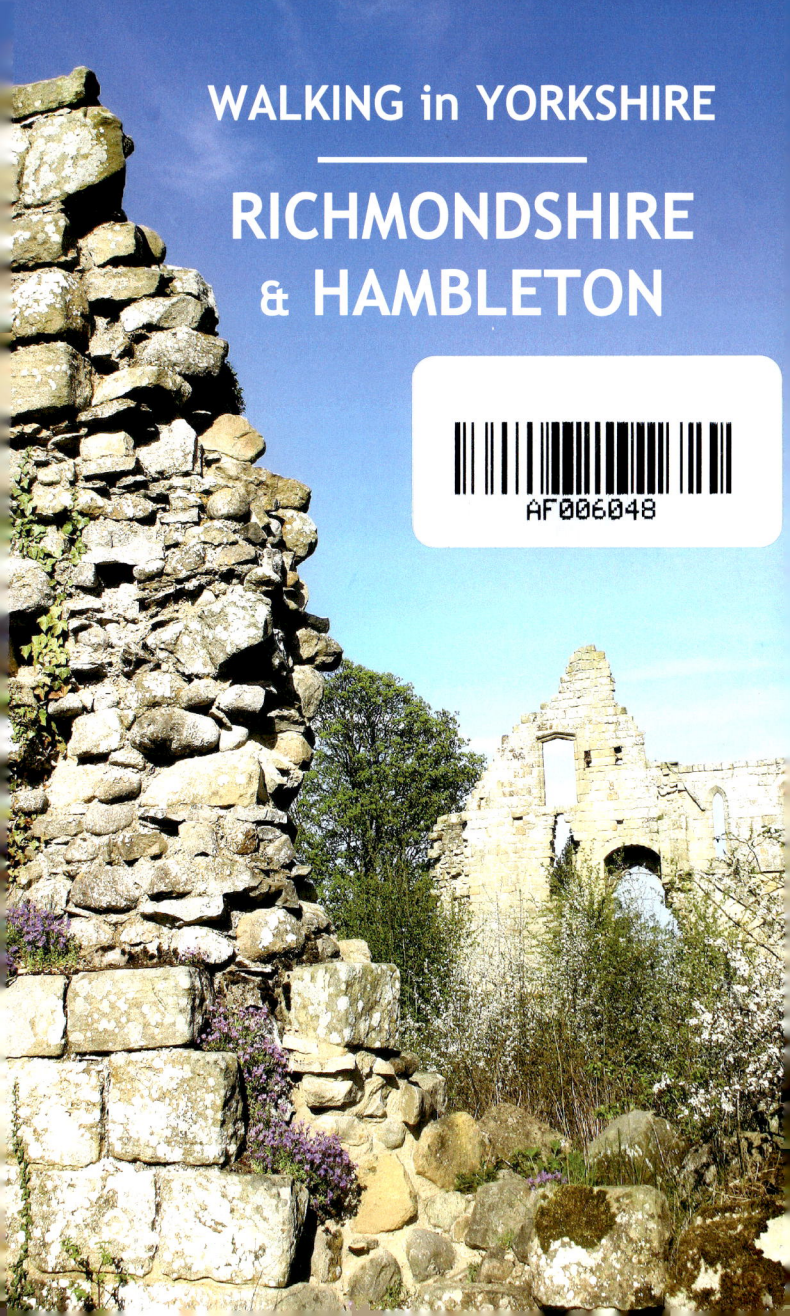

WALKING in YORKSHIRE

RICHMONDSHIRE & HAMBLETON

HILLSIDE GUIDES - ACROSS THE NORTH

Yorkshire River Photobook •JOURNEY OF THE WHARFE

Hillwalking •MOUNTAINS OF THE YORKSHIRE DALES

Easy Walks •50 YORKSHIRE WALKS FOR ALL

Walking in Yorkshire - North/East (25 Walks)
- HOWARDIAN HILLS & VALE OF YORK
- YORKSHIRE WOLDS
- NORTH YORK MOORS South/West
- NORTH YORK MOORS North/East
- RICHMONDSHIRE & HAMBLETON

Walking in Yorkshire - West/South/Mid (25 Walks)
- AIRE VALLEY & BRONTE COUNTRY
- HARROGATE & ILKLEY
- CALDERDALE & SOUTH PENNINES
- SOUTH YORKSHIRE
- WEST YORKSHIRE COUNTRYSIDE

Walking in Yorkshire - Yorkshire Dales (25 Walks)
- East: NIDDERDALE & RIPON
- West: THREE PEAKS & HOWGILL FELLS
- South: WHARFEDALE & MALHAM
- North: WENSLEYDALE & SWALEDALE

Lancashire/Cumbria •PENDLE & the RIBBLE •EDEN VALLEY

Long Distance Walks
- COAST TO COAST WALK
- DALES WAY
- CUMBRIA WAY
- PENDLE WAY

Hillwalking - Lake District (25 Walks)
- LAKELAND FELLS - SOUTH
- LAKELAND FELLS - EAST
- LAKELAND FELLS - NORTH
- LAKELAND FELLS - WEST

Short Scenic Walks - Yorkshire (30 Walks)
- WENSLEYDALE
- WHARFEDALE & ILKLEY
- NORTH YORK MOORS
- THREE PEAKS & MALHAM
- HARROGATE & NIDDERDALE
- HAWORTH & AIRE VALLEY
- SOUTH PENNINES

Short Scenic Walks - Lancashire/Cumbria/Durham (30 Walks)
- RIBBLE VALLEY & BOWLAND
- PENDLE & LANCASHIRE MOORS
- AMBLESIDE & SOUTH LAKELAND
- ARNSIDE & LUNESDALE
- TEESDALE & WEARDALE

Send for a detailed current catalogue and price list and also visit www.hillsidepublications.co.uk

WALKING in YORKSHIRE

RICHMONDSHIRE & HAMBLETON

Paul Hannon

Hillside

HILLSIDE PUBLICATIONS

38 Westburn Avenue
Keighley
West Yorkshire
BD22 6AW

First published 2024

© Paul Hannon 2024   ISBN 978-1-907626-31-9

Cover illustrations: Carlton Moor; Richmond; Aldbrough St John
Page One: Jervaulx Abbey; Page Three: Ainderby Steeple
Above: River Ure, Ulshaw Bridge; Opposite: Thirsk
(Paul Hannon/Yorkshire Photo Library)

The sketch maps are based on 1947 Ordnance Survey One-Inch maps

Printed in China on behalf of Latitude Press

Whilst the author has walked and researched all the routes for the purposes of this guide, no responsibility can be accepted for any unforeseen circumstances encountered while following them. The publisher would appreciate information regarding material changes.

CONTENTS

INTRODUCTION..................6

THE WALKS (mileage in brackets)
1 Easby Abbey (5¾)...............10
2 Hudswell Woods (5½)..........13
3 Wensley & River Ure (6½).....16
4 Middleham Low Moor (7½).....20
5 Jervaulx Abbey (7½)...........24
6 Constable Burton (6¾).........28
7 Crakehall (5½)..................32
8 Thornborough Henges (6¼)....35
9 Snape Park & Well (6¼)........38
10 Around Pickhill (7)..............42
11 Cod Beck & Sowerby (5¾).....46
12 Around Felixkirk (7¼)..........50
13 Borrowby Banks (6)............54
14 Around the Siltons (5¼).......57
15 Scarth Wood Moor (6).........60
16 Carlton Moor (6¼)..............64
17 Above the Leven (5¾).........67
18 River Wiske (5¾)...............70
19 Coast to Coast Walk (6).......73
20 River Swale (5½)...............76
21 Fleetham & Fencotes (5¼)....79
22 Bolton-on-Swale (6¼).........82
23 Hartforth & Whashton (6).....85
24 Kirby Hill & Dalton (6¼).......88
25 Stanwick Fort (6¼).............92

INDEX.................................96

INTRODUCTION

The two historic districts of Richmondshire and Hambleton combine to occupy a massive swathe of rural North Yorkshire. The county's two outstanding national parks, the Yorkshire Dales and the North York Moors, are the magnificent bookends to this area, framing the Vale of Mowbray which occupies a vast low-level tract at the heart of God's Own Country. The irrepressible rivers Swale and Ure retain their charms as they prepare to leave the Dales, and their lovely banks feature in several of the walks. Similarly, to the east, the North York Moors boasts heather-draped moorland gazing out over the plains, perched loftily above the delectable villages of Osmotherley, Boltby and Carlton.

It must be conceded that much of the central section is far from prime walking country, yet research reveals pleasurable routes and ample interest in amongst an admittedly intensively farmed landscape. Several potential routes had to be discarded due to unfavourable conditions, be it summer nettles or simply non-existent paths and tiresome arable field crossings. But those that survived the cull are worth the effort in representing this vast expanse of Yorkshire. Even then, the surviving walks might still inflict uncomfortable moments on shorts-wearers in high summer.

Overall the landscape of this book's remit is incredibly varied. In addition to the uplands of the Dales and Moors, you have a range of intriguing features. The market towns of Bedale, Leyburn and Thirsk each play host to a walk and each merits a day's leisurely exploration, while countless shy villages have charming cottages set back from sweeping greens. Historical gems include majestic castles at Richmond, Middleham and Snape; atmospheric abbeys at Jervaulx and Easby; and ancient earthworks at Thornborough, Stanwick and Castle Steads. Historic churches of note include Well, Kirby Hill, Felixkirk and Stanwick St John, with grand houses at Crakehall, Braithwaite Hall and Hartforth. Capacious village greens are found at Hutton Rudby, Aldbrough St John, Ravensworth and East Witton; old mills at Kilvington, Crathorne and Crakehall; while inspirational nature reserves occupy old mineral workings at Scorton and Nosterfield. The Wensleydale Railway is a notable attraction, and then there is Richmond, very much the jewel in the crown.

INTRODUCTION

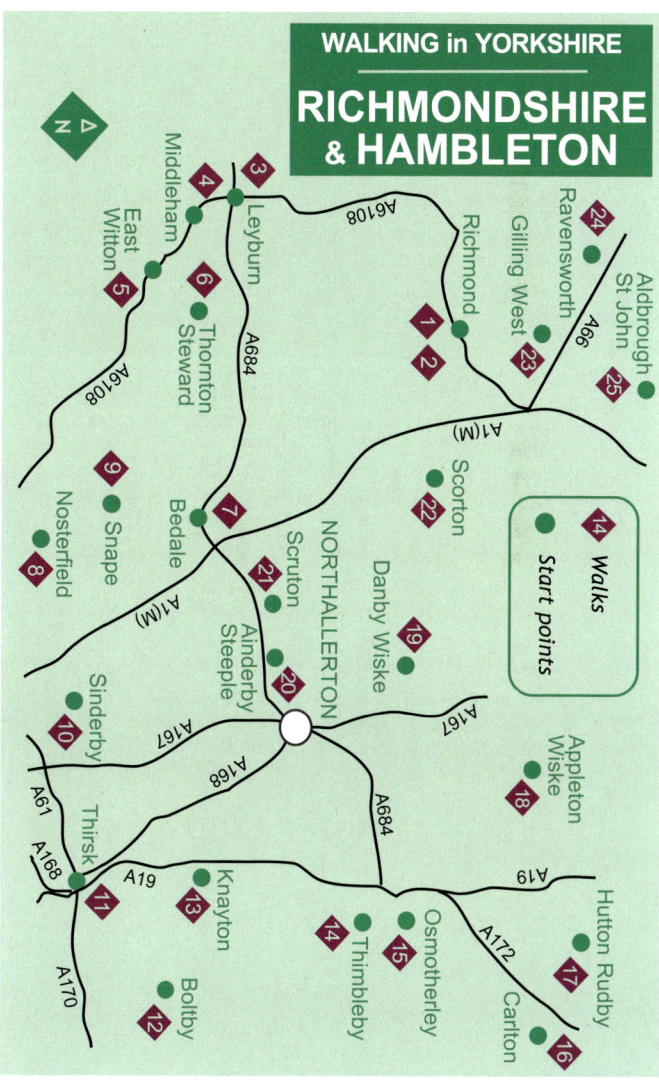

INTRODUCTION

Richmond is the gateway to Swaledale, a remarkable town steeped in history and dominated by the castle on its promontory above the Swale. Begun in 1071, its enormous 12th century keep watches over the whole town. The equally enormous Market Place has in the centre of its sloping cobbles Holy Trinity church with a 14th century tower: it incorporates the Green Howards Museum. Lined by shops, pubs and cafes, the Market Place serves as a bus station as well as its original purpose on Saturdays: a market cross is still very much in evidence. Outside of the square from which numerous wynds (narrow ways) radiate is St Mary's church with a 14th century tower. Grey Friars Tower stands across from the still functioning Georgian Theatre of 1788, while the revitalised former station has a wealth of attractions. The military presence around town is due to the proximity of Catterick Camp.

Using the guide

The walks range from $5^1/_4$ to $7^1/_2$ miles, the average distance being around $6^1/_4$ miles. Each walk is self-contained, with essential information being followed by a concise route description and a simple map. Dovetailed in between are snippets of information on features along the way: these are placed in *italics* to ensure that the all important route description is easier to locate. Start point postcodes are a rough guide for those with 'satnav': grid references are more precise! Though bus services within the area are limited, availability, if any, is mentioned in the introduction to each walk.

INTRODUCTION

The sketch maps serve to identify the location of the routes rather than the fine detail, and whilst the description should be sufficient to guide you around, the appropriate Ordnance Survey map is recommended. To gain the most from a walk, the detail of a 1:25,000 scale Explorer map is unsurpassed. It also gives the option to vary walks as desired, giving a much improved picture of your surroundings and the availability of any linking paths for shortening or lengthening walks. Five maps cover all the walks:
- *Explorer OL26 - North York Moors, West (5 walks)*
- *Explorer OL30 - Yorkshire Dales, North/Central (2 walks)*
- *Explorer 299 - Ripon & Boroughbridge (1 walk)*
- *Explorer 302 - Northallerton & Thirsk (11 walks)*
- *Explorer 304 - Darlington & Richmond (7 walks)*

Also useful for planning are Landranger maps 92, 93, 99 and 100.

Visitor Information
Market Hall, Market Place **Richmond** DL10 4QL • 01748-826468
93A Market Place **Thirsk** YO7 1EY • 01845-522755
Westgarth **Northallerton** DL7 8NA • 01609-776864
Bedale Hall Community Centre **Bedale** DL8 1AA • 01677-424604

Opposite: Carlton-in-Cleveland   *Wensleydale Railway*

WALK 1 EASBY ABBEY

A magnificent monastic ruin amid good spells with the Swale

START *Richmond (NZ 171008; DL10 4QL)*

DISTANCE *5¾ miles (9¼km)*

ORDNANCE SURVEY 1:25,000 MAP
Explorer 304 - Darlington & Richmond

ACCESS *Start from the town centre, car parks. Bus from Ripon, Leyburn, Darlington, Barnard Castle, Keld, Northallerton.*

For a note on Richmond, see page 8. From the south-west corner of Market Place descend New Road, within yards bearing left on a cobbled way (The Bar) that drops beneath an arch onto Bridge Street. *The arch was part of 14th century town walls.* Go left to a junction at The Green. *On the corner is a pair of sundials from 1721.* Go left over the Swale on Richmond Bridge (Green Bridge), looking back at a classic castle view. Briefly ascend the roadside footway then take narrow Boggy Lane right, on its hollowed course up to a house. A grassy way passes to its left to a stile where it rises away encased in greenery, levelling out for a good stroll, at the end swinging left to join a road. Go briefly left to a bridle-gate in the hedge on the right, and a super path drops away between greenery. At the bottom things open out to drop left across a scrubby bank to run to a bridle-gate onto a road junction at Sandbeck House.

EASBY ABBEY • WALK 1

Cross to the side road rising into woodland to reach the drive to Holly House Farm. Go left the short way to the holiday cottages, and a bridle-gate at the far end. A faint path heads directly away to a corner of West Wood, continuing more clearly outside it. Beyond it, continue to a gate and on again to one onto a road alongside Woodhouse Farm on your left. Go very briefly right to a junction with the A6136, and equally briefly left on its footway to a path on the right. Across a parallel pathway, pass through a gate set back, and head away on a grassy cart track with a fence to a gate ahead. Now bear right on a thin trod over the sloping sheep pasture to a gate. *Big views look across the Vale of Mowbray to the Hambleton Hills.*

Advance on across two more pastures linked by a gate, and faced with a pair of gates use the left one to follow a fence on your right to drop to a kissing-gate into Park Wood. A path drops to a bridge on a stream and

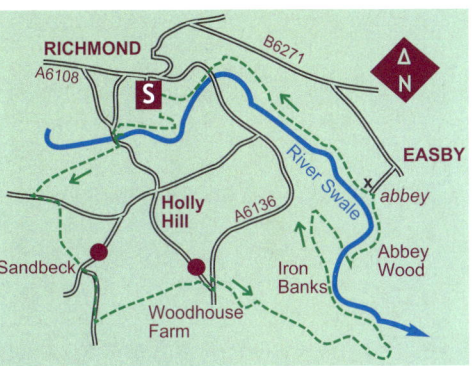

up the other side to a kissing-gate back out. Rise over the brow with a hedge to your right, dropping gently to meet a track. Go left on this just a few yards to a path junction at the site of Hagg Farm.

Double back left on a thin path that rapidly becomes clearer: it runs a short level course above a scrubby bank to a metal kissing-gate into woodland at Iron Banks. The path runs on to slant down to the river. This is traced upstream through trees, encountering a footbridge on a sidestream and enjoying a characterful river bend before a kissing-gate out into a sloping pasture. The path runs on past sewage works to meet its access road: just yards further, join the old railway track on your right. *This was the final mile of the Richmond branch line that opened in 1846 and closed in 1969.* Double back right the short way to its bridge on the Swale, a super vantage point. Across, double back left on a driveway, shadowing

WALK 1 • EASBY ABBEY

the river to the hamlet of Easby, dominated by its beautiful abbey ruins. *The Premonstratensian abbey was founded in 1152 by Roald, the Constable of Richmond Castle. In its shadow, St Agatha's church dates from the 12th century, and features 13th century wall paintings discovered during Victorian restoration work.*

Resume on the short driveway left of the abbey, passing the entrance to end at a house. An enclosed path to its left quickly emerges into a field, go left to a kissing-gate into riverbank trees. Within yards the path forks: take that down steps to the river, and follow it upstream amid nice surrounds. At the end it joins a rough access road alongside the Drummer Boy's Stone. *A plaque recounts the associated legend.* Go left on the road, rising above the river and running on to emerge onto Lombards Wynd back in town. Go left the few strides to the A6136, crossing to a surfaced path into the grassy spaces of The Batts. When the main path slants uphill, take one going left to the river at Richmond Falls. Leave through the adjacent car park/WC and up the road to the right, climbing back into town with the castle keep hovering above. Part way up, double back left along the front of Castle Terrace, and a surfaced path swings round to the Castle Walk, a splendid terrace with great river views from the base of the castle walls. At the end it curves around to re-enter the centre where you left it.

Easby Abbey

HUDSWELL WOODS

WALK 2

Rich woodland and lush pastures above the River Swale

START Richmond (NZ 171008; DL10 4QL)

DISTANCE 5½ miles (8¾km)

ORDNANCE SURVEY 1:25,000 MAP
Explorer 304 - Darlington & Richmond

ACCESS Start from the town centre, car parks. Bus from Ripon, Leyburn, Darlington, Barnard Castle, Keld, Northallerton.

For a note on Richmond, see page 8. From the south-west corner of Market Place descend New Road, within yards bearing left on a cobbled way (The Bar) that drops beneath an arch onto Bridge Street. *The arch was part of 14th century town walls.* Go left to a junction at The Green. *Note on the corner here a pair of sundials from 1721.* Go left to cross the Swale on Richmond Bridge (Green Bridge), looking back at a classic castle view. Immediately across take a broad path upstream into woodland. *Over the river is Culloden Tower, a mid-18th century folly that is now a holiday let.* At an early fork keep left, a broad path slanting gently up through Billy Bank Wood. Beneath a big quarried face and then a long line of smaller crags, you reach a bend looking down on a river bend. Here a stepped option drops to the bank to resume upstream, but it's easier to resume through the trees, soon slanting more gently

WALK 2 • HUDSWELL WOODS

down to a kissing-gate into a riverside pasture. Cross to a path by the river and go left on a splendid broad green way, becoming firmer as wooded slopes closer in to reach (but not cross) a footbridge on the Swale accessing Round Howe car park/WC.

Ignoring the bridge and other paths, resume upstream through Hudswell Woods, dropping down a few early steps to regain the actual bank. An encounter with a sandy beach precedes the finest section in company with the river. Past an old quarry a fork is reached: take the left one, slanting gently up to mid-height and passing beneath substantial cliffs. Further, at a fork, ignore the right branch dropping to the river and keep on a little further to reach the daunting Hudswell Steps just short of the wood edge. Cross straight over to a small gate beyond, out of the wood.

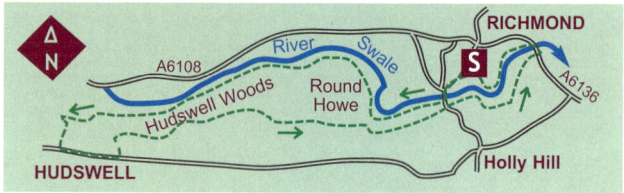

A path heads away, slanting gently on and enjoying open views from scrubby slopes. Reaching a junction with a path slanting down from the left, and with your current path maintaining that slant down to a gate ahead, opt to double back left up this path, raking pleasantly across the slope to meet a higher path. A cross-paths with Hudswell Steps is just ahead, and you could simply remain on the wood-top. For variety, opt for the 32-step rise into a field, and ascend a grassy path to a small gate at the top. This sends an enclosed path to the road in Hudswell. Go left on the footway, past the award-winning George & Dragon with a little shop attached.

A little beyond the village hall, take a gap on the left to a gate/stile into a field, and descend to a gate/gap in the corner below. A path drops down through scrub into a clearing, and forks. Back in the wood top, take the right-hand path dropping briefly through scrub onto a level wood-top path. Turn right to immediately cross a mini ravine to commence a largely level stroll above steep wooded slopes. Soon you ascend 13 wooden steps to resume along a field outside the wood. Go left through a bridle-gate to another

HUDSWELL WOODS • WALK 2

back into the trees. Resume as before, soon reaching a fork. This time take the small gate out of the trees into open pasture.

Angle away to a bridle-gate in a hedge, then on with the hedge to one at the end. Cross an open area to another into the wood top, soon reaching a stile back out and across a field corner to a hedge-stile. A very brief enclosed section leads to a stile into a field, and along to another in a hedge just ahead. Cross to one ahead and resume to a bridle-gate back into trees, with a little gate rapidly back out. Curve round the wood edge a little further, but before the corner bear right to a hedge-stile ahead. Bear right to another, then cross between slim enclosures before slanting slightly right through two further stiles to one into a larger equestrian pasture.

Bear very slightly right across to a dip where the wood comes up. Over a stile here, a path forms to run to a stile back into trees: ignore it and keep on the grass path above the wood to a corner kissing-gate. A firm path enters the trees, and the river re-appears beneath an exceedingly steep drop. The path runs along the top before slanting down a part sunken way to emerge onto the road on the other side of the house where you left it by the bridge.

Cross the road, not the bridge, to the football club at Earl's Orchard. A path passes left of the clubhouse to run by the river to reach a fork: take the main one rising to a kissing-gate into South Bank Fields. *The ensuing path through these wildflower meadows is a concession one courtesy of Richmondshire Landscape Trust.* Take the path left, outside the trees and opening out along the base of the meadow to a bridle-gate. With fine views across to the castle keep, it continues through two further meadows to Station Bridge. *Constructed in 1846 to connect the town to its new railway station, it was renamed Mercury Bridge in 1975.*

Pass under to ascend steps to the bridge alongside the Old Station with its various attractions. Across the bridge take a path left into the grassy spaces of The Batts. When the main path slants uphill, take one going left to the river at Richmond Falls. Leave through the adjacent car park/WC and up the road to the right, climbing back into town with the castle keep hovering above. Part way up, double back left along the front of Castle Terrace, and a surfaced path swings round to the Castle Walk, a splendid terrace with great river views from the base of the castle walls. At the end it curves around to re-enter the centre where you left it.

WALK 3: WENSLEY & RIVER URE

Excellent paths to two fine villages linked by the River Ure

START Leyburn (SE 112904; DL8 5AS)

DISTANCE 6½ miles (10½km)

ORDNANCE SURVEY 1:25,000 MAP
Explorer OL30 - Yorkshire Dales North/Central

ACCESS *Start from the market square in the centre, ample parking. Bus from Ripon, Richmond, Masham and Hawes*

The busy little town of Leyburn is Wensleydale's true gateway. A vast market place fulfils its original function on Fridays, when dalesfolk from miles around add further colour to the scene. At the top stands the imposing town hall of 1856, while pubs, cafes and shops do brisk trade. Just off the market place are 18th century Leyburn Hall, Thornborough Hall, St Matthew's church of 1868, and a Roman Catholic church dating back to 1835. Leyburn is also proud home to the ever popular Wensleydale Show in late August. From the mini-roundabout at the top of town go left on the Hawes road, dropping rapidly out of town onto a parallel footway the short way to the last house. As a rough access road drops away, instead take a stile by a gate alongside, and slant down the field. Through old gateposts advance on to stiles either side of the Wensleydale Railway.

WENSLEY & RIVER URE • WALK 3

This was a 40-mile link between the Vale of York and the Pennines, reaching Hawes in 1878 and on to Garsdale Head (then known as Hawes Junction) where it met the Settle-Carlisle line. The last passenger service ran in 1954, and the rails were removed above Redmire in 1965. The lower 22 miles remained to serve a quarry above Redmire, but in 1992 this ceased and only an occasional military train brought armoured vehicles towards Catterick Garrison. A campaign to save the line has made good progress, with passenger services re-starting in 2003 from Leeming Bar as far as Leyburn. Extended to Redmire just a year later, at the time of research this final section has been unworkable due to the old track requiring upgrading.

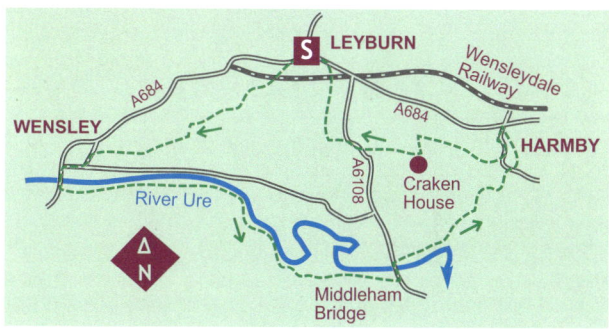

From a small gate just behind, continue to a stile by a barn, then head away with a fence on your right. *Ahead, Penhill looks magnificent throughout this stage, with Braithwaite Moor to your left.* This remains your course along several fieldsides, aiming towards Penhill. Passing a renovated house, a few open strides precede resuming along fieldsides, until the adjacent wall swings sharp left. Stay with it until after it turns off, and just a short way further taker a stile in the replacement fence. Head directly away to one ahead into Leyburn Old Glebe nature reserve: a path drops gently to a streamlet footbridge then up to a small gate back out. Go left to a kissing-gate into a large, sloping pasture, a faint path dropping down across it to a kissing-gate in the far corner. A path runs to a stile just ahead, then along the bottom of a long field to a wall-stile at the end. Advance on beneath a large house to a bridle-gate onto a back road in Wensley. Drop left onto Low Lane, then right the short way to the central junction with the A684.

WALK 3 • WENSLEY & RIVER URE

Wensley is a hugely attractive village, largely out of character with the typical Dales villages upstream. This is partly due to the fact that this once important market town (a charter was granted in 1202) that gave its name to the dale was decimated by the Plague in 1563, and never recovered its status. Holy Trinity church has various Scrope memorials, including their 17th century family pew: also of interest is a 16th century rood screen. The graceful bridge dates back to the 15th century, though since enlarged. Village pub is the Three Horseshoes, while visitors are welcome at a candle-makers in the old mill.

Leave by turning left on the footway down to Wensley Bridge on the River Ure. Across, pass through a gate/gap on the left with another just below, and head downstream on a grassy riverbank track by the wide-flowing river. This course is followed for a considerable time, later narrowing to a path. Initially with scrub partly hiding the river, things later open out for an even better stroll. Shortly after passing a second pine plantation strip, the river makes a big swing left, and you reach a few trees. Here bear right to a farm bridge on a streamlet, and bear right across an open field, away from the river to join a firm track. Follow this left to quickly rejoin the river, and becoming enclosed it runs on by a couple of houses and out on their access road onto the A6108.

Go briefly left to cross Middleham Bridge. *Originally a suspension bridge, its imposing double castellated arches of 1830 were repaired in 1865.* Across it take a gate on the right and head away across the field centre, parallel with the nearby river. Through a gate/stile at the end a tractor track heads away, crossing a farm bridge on a streamlet with a neat little arched bridge alongside. Advance to a gate ahead, and a firm track rises outside new tree plantings. As it fades, bear right to a corner wall-stile. Now slant left up to another by the top corner onto Throstle Nest Farm's access road. Go right to a cattle-grid, across which the unseen right of way bears gently left to cut a corner of the road before rejoining it. Just ahead is another cattle-grid at a junction, where go left the short way onto the road in the village of Harmby. *On your left is a former Wesleyan Methodist Chapel of 1855, and on your right is the village hall.*

Just a few yards to the right turn up suburban Hargill, and just around the bend at the top, a snicket rises between gardens into a field. A little path bears left around the corner to a gate/stile into woodland enclosing Harmby Beck. The path rises gently right to quickly reach Harmby Falls, with delectable waterfalls below and above a footbridge.

WENSLEY & RIVER URE • WALK 3

Across the bridge double back downstream, the path quickly rising onto a road in the village. *Just up to the right is the Pheasant Inn on the main road.* Drop left almost to the point you entered, but just past the phonebox go right on a short access road at Harmby Manor Garth. Becoming an equally short cart track at a gate/stile, advance to gates just ahead. Take the small gate sending an enclosed path along to emerge into a field at an information panel. A splendid green path heads across two sloping fields to bridge a sidestream and reach a rough access road. Turn down this between two houses to end at Craken House Farm caravan site. Turn sharp right on the access road which runs out across a field to emerge onto the A6108.

Turn briefly right on the verge, soon crossing to a kissing-gate opposite. Head away across three slim fields, then turn right up the next field to join a grass track rising parallel with a hedge. Through a gate/stile continue up to join a rough access road at the top right, running briefly out onto a suburban street. Just a few yards to the right, a surfaced path rises between gardens, and continues up to cross an access road at the top. Wooden steps take you back up onto the road, crossing a railway bridge to rise back into the centre opposite the church.

Middleham from near Harmby

WALK 4
MIDDLEHAM LOW MOOR

The environs of Middleham and lower Coverdale provide a rich wealth of historic interest and outstanding views

START Middleham (SE 127877; DL8 4NP)

DISTANCE 7½ miles (12km)

ORDNANCE SURVEY 1:25,000 MAP
Explorer OL30 - Yorkshire Dales North/Central

ACCESS Start from the town centre. Parking in square and higher up nearer castle. Ripon-Leyburn bus.

    Middleham is an absorbing place: a village in size perhaps, but unquestionably a town in stature. It is famous for both its horse racing connections (numerous stables nearby) and its castle, and is the historic gateway to Wensleydale. The castle's finest features are the massive Norman keep and 14th century gatehouse. It was for centuries the stronghold of the Nevilles, and known as the 'Windsor of the North'. Richard, Earl of Warwick - the King-maker - lived here, and his daughter married Richard, Duke of Gloucester, later to become its most famous resident, the much maligned Richard III. It is maintained by English Heritage. A cross at the head of the town recalls the grant obtained in 1479 for a twice-yearly fair and market by Richard, when Duke of Gloucester. Alongside are a fountain, the old school of 1869, and a sundial of 1778. The church of St Mary & St Alkelda dates from the 14th century, and

MIDDLEHAM LOW MOOR • WALK 4

includes a monument to Abbott Robert Thornton of Jervaulx. Centrepiece today is the small sloping square, with a market cross on tiered steps and several pubs, a shop and tearooms.

Leave the main street by making for the castle, to the left of which an enclosed track runs outside the castle walls. *Just short of a gate at the end, consider a detour from a stile on the right. From it slant up a field to a fence-gate, continuing up to the prominent William's Hill. This wooded knoll is the site of a 'ring and bailey', where a timber castle long preceded the main attraction below. It consists of an outer bank, ditch and inner bank, containing a level centrepiece where a 40ft high motte stood.*

Back on the lane, pass through the gate and a grassy way rises directly up the wallside with views back over the castle. Over the brow it drops down to a gate/stile to resume down the other side. *Ahead, the deep trough of the River Cover is backed by Braithwaite Moor, with the mighty Penhill further right.*

At the start of a wooded side gill on your left, a path starts to drop more steeply to Cover Banks: just a little further, take a lesser, clear path contouring to the right. Joining a broader one outside a wooded bank, go right to rise gently to a corner. Twin stiles on the left take you through the edge of a small pinewood, then the path slants down a nice unkempt pasture. At the bottom continue along a field edge outside the trees, and part way on it slants down the bank to the River Cover. Go right along this short pasture to a stile at stone-arched Hullo Bridge set amid splendid scenery. Cross and linger at this lovely spot as the river carves a modest ravine and flows over a slabby limestone bed.

Head away on a grassy bridleway slanting right up the bank. It then rises more gently, on through a gate and faintly along to a gate onto a minor road opposite Braithwaite Hall. *This imposing*

WALK 4 • MIDDLEHAM LOW MOOR

17th century farmhouse is in the care of the National Trust, open to visitors in summer months by prior arrangement. Turn right for a few minutes to a stile/gate on the left. An intermittent green way slants away, gradually rising across vast Hanghow Pastures, aiming for the top of a stand of pines. *In the valley is Coverham church, while Penhill rises ahead.* Later levelling, it runs past the trees to rise imperceptibly further to a fence-gate. Cross to a wall-gate in a recess ahead, and a grassy path advances on with a wall.

First however, take a few minutes' detour to Castle Steads, an Iron Age hillfort just up to the left. Rise briefly up rougher pasture, then through some bracken to emerge onto the site beneath the moor-edge wall. *Sat on a level shelf, distinctive grassy ditches and banks defend three sides of it. Features of the view range from the distant North York Moors to the much closer Pinker's Pond under Middleham Low Moor.* Turn right on a broad green way along its crest, slanting down at the end to fade but pointing you back onto the path in the bottom corner. Through the small gate the way advances on with the wall, soon becoming a firmer track as it curves left and runs on to merge with a house drive. This continues along before dropping at the end to a gate into Caldbergh, a sleepy Coverdale hamlet of attractive cottages.

Drop down this short access road onto a through road, and turn right for a level ten minutes. *At a kink note a fine limekiln up to the right beneath an old quarry.* A little after a roadside barn, bear left down a narrow enclosed pathway, dropping at the bottom to a tall footbridge over the tree-lined Cover. Across, the path slants gently right up the bank to Bird Ridding Farm's access road. Go right the short way out onto a road. Turn very briefly right, then left up the access road for Tupgill Park and the Forbidden Corner. With broad verges it rises amid park-like surrounds, keeping right at a fork where the left branch goes up to the attractive house of Tupgill Park. A crossroads is reached with the Forbidden Corner to your left. *This visitor attraction features gardens and intriguing follies, along with a restaurant and café.*

Your route advances straight on through ornate gates, rising past an attractive pond in the grounds of Ferngill. *Alongside it is the Fishing Temple, built in 1910 as a box in which horses relaxed by 'paddling' in the water it contained.* Follow the drive up to the house, and straight past it to quickly pass through large gateposts

MIDDLEHAM LOW MOOR • WALK 4

to emerge onto grassy Middleham Low Moor. *Middleham Low Moor is renowned as a venue for exercising racehorses. Although Open Access land, be aware of their possible presence. Mornings are the time to witness these elegant creatures being put through their paces, and dogs should be on a lead if here then.*

Turn right along a firm access road, but quickly bear left across short-cropped grass, soon meeting a level grassy track. Go right on this, running parallel with the road as you stride across the moor, just this side of the broad brow. Gradually narrowing, it encounters a dip and a rise before fading. Ideally bear left towards the lengthy rails that appear on the gallops, and shadow them on a very long, gentle decline. *Looking back right, Little Whernside and Great Whernside rise at the distant head of Coverdale.*

Descend parallel with the fence, maintaining this line down to an open road. Cross to a parallel path and go left to where the road becomes enclosed. Here a stile in the wall on the right sends a path dropping left along a fieldside, through an intervening stile and down to a small gate into a horse paddock. Maintain this line to a bridle-gate just short of the far corner, with the castle dominant alongside. A short path crosses an unkempt corner to a stile back onto the track where you began.

Middleham Castle

WALK 5
JERVAULX ABBEY

Monastic ruins in a beautiful setting, two old villages and a delectable stretch of the River Ure in lower Wensleydale

START *East Witton (SE 144860; DL8 4SN)*

DISTANCE *7½ miles (12km)*

ORDNANCE SURVEY 1:25,000 MAP
Explorer 302 - Northallerton & Thirsk

ACCESS *Start from the village centre, roadside parking. Leyburn-Masham bus*

East Witton suffered terribly in the plague of 1563, and was rebuilt as an estate village by the Earl of Ailesbury at the start of the 19th century. The church of St John the Evangelist, built in 1809, stands just east of the village. Two lines of houses are set back from a vast, sweeping green, while at the crossroads stands the Blue Lion pub, as well as an attractive former school. From the crossroads adjacent to the main road at the east end of the village, head south along Lowthorpe, swinging left and leaving the houses to pass a burial ground en route to Waterloo farm. Bear right past the large barns and along the continuing access road. Running to bridge Parson's Beck, it climbs to end at Thirsting Castle Lodge.

Go straight on over the bridge on lively Deep Gill Beck, and go right on the continuing track outside its wooded confines. This quickly doubles back left through a gate and briefly steeply up the field. *Big views look over to Leyburn under a moorland skyline, with Danby Hall across the valley.* Levelling out it swings left to another gate, then right with a fence to a track junction near the rear of Hammer Farm. Through the gate to your left, cross to another at the right of the farm buildings, joining its driveway by the house at the front. *A 'permissible alternative' avoids the farm by staying on the track the short way up to a firmer, level one. Go briefly left then drop down to join the drive.* Now simply follow the level drive (Hammer Road) out along a defined shelf. *Long views look over the lower valley to the distant Hambleton Hills.*

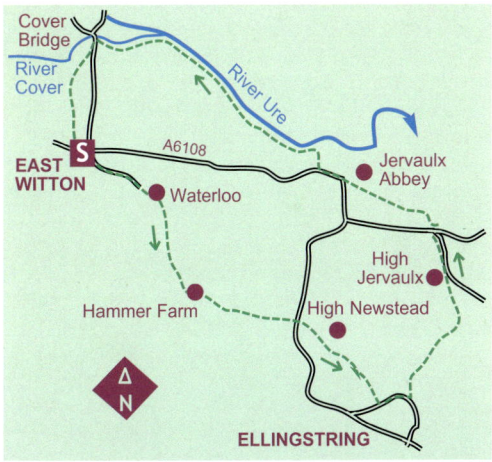

At the end cross Stark Bank Road onto High Newstead farm drive, then from a stile on the right cross the field to a bridle-gate in the top corner. Maintain the slant to a small gate in the fence ahead, looking down on the farm. Slant again to a top corner stile onto a surfaced access road, and ignoring a stile opposite, go very briefly left to meet an ascending enclosed path. Turn right up its sunken course, soon levelling out to approach a bend where take a stile on the left. Cross the field to farm buildings: entering at a gate, turn right up the near side into a small enclosure. At its top right corner a short enclosed path runs out to emerge onto the street in Ellingstring, the highest point of the walk.

WALK 5 • JERVAULX ABBEY

Ellingstring is a lovely little village, well off the beaten track and sheltering beneath the edge of extensive moorland. Just to the right is a sloping green with seats and daffodils, while the old school retains its bell. Here also is a former Wesleyan Methodist chapel of 1848. Turn left to a minor dip, and leave by a rough road left just before the phonebox. Forking in front of a barn, take the left branch's hedgerowed course, soon dropping to a sharp bend. Take a gate in front just before the track ends, and bear right to an early bridle-gate. Bear left away from it through a scant hedge, maintaining the slant down to an outer fence corner. Continue down with the fence, and levelling out to approach a bridle-gate at the end, instead drop left to a ladder-stile over the wall just below. Head away with a tall hedge to a stile onto the A6108 by the drive to High Jervaulx. *This is the home of Brymor ice cream, with cafe.*

Without joining the road, a bridle-gate across the driveway sends a permissive fieldside path parallel with the road, dropping all the way to a similar gate by a junction at the bottom. Cross to a cattle-grid alongside a lodge to enter tranquil Jervaulx Park. A grass track heads away left to join a firmer track, but the right of way bears left off the track, keeping a little higher as it runs to an outer fence corner containing a couple of houses. With Jervaulx Abbey appearing ahead, advance on to merge into the track close by the abbey. *The abbey is in private hands, with a honesty box by the entrance. It was founded by Cistercian monks in 1156, having originated from Byland Abbey, and briefly set up near Aysgarth a decade earlier. The name derives from Yore Vale, Yore being the old name for the Ure. At the Dissolution in 1536, much of its stone was plundered for building, but these remain very romantic ruins.*

JERVAULX ABBEY • WALK 5

The carriageway crosses the abbey visitors' path to a cattle-grid in front of Jervaulx Hall, going left on a short drive back out onto the A6108. Turn right for a few minutes on a grassy verge, and after bridging a beck, take a fieldside track right to the bank of the River Ure. Turn left, commencing a magical stroll upstream close to the lush grassy bank. *The prow of Penhill appears up-dale, with an early glimpse of Danby Hall across the river.* The finest section ends at a bridle-gate alongside a reedy pond. The path runs on with woodland to the left, passing a riverbank viewpoint for the hall. A little further note the former Danby Low Mill on the opposite bank, then just beyond a gate, the confluence of Ure and Cover is seen. The latter river leads the final stage to Cover Bridge. *Across this fine arched bridge stands the welcoming Cover Bridge Inn.*

The route simply crosses the road, not the bridge, with stone steps back down onto the bank. Cross to a small gate onto the bank opposite the pub, but instead of following the river, stay with the hedge as it curves left. Through a gate just short of the tapering end, advance to another gate just ahead. Cross to a fence-gate and on to a stile left of a large modern barn. From a stile round the back go left with the wall, maintaining this line over streamlets and stiles until a minor brow reveals East Witton. In a smaller enclosure take a gap-stile on the left at the end of the hedge, and head along the last field to emerge back into the village alongside a former Methodist chapel of 1882.

Opposite: River Ure   *Jervaulx Abbey*

WALK 6
CONSTABLE BURTON

Two pleasant villages linked by a charming beck

START Thornton Steward (SE 180878; HG4 4GB)

DISTANCE 6¾ miles (10¾km)

ORDNANCE SURVEY 1:25,000 MAP
Explorer 302 - Northallerton & Thirsk

ACCESS Start from Yorkshire Water's car park at Thornton Steward Reservoir, north of village.

Thornton Steward Reservoir was completed as recently as 1976, and holds some 218 million gallons. Set in a curious upland bowl, it is used by both fishing and sailing clubs. Enter the confines of the reservoir and head left past the sailing clubhouse and boats. At the end a broad grassy way rises gently above the reservoir's gorse bank, with a hedge to your left. At the high point just ahead the fence drops away, but the way continues along the brow. *The reservoir forms a foreground to the distant Cleveland Hills and Hambleton Hills across the Vale of Mowbray. The shapelier profile of Penhill overlooks Wensleydale to your left.*

Over a minor dip rise towards the wooded knoll ahead, where a bridle-gate set back to its left ushers you out of the reservoir environs. A hedgeside path heads away, dropping to bridge a stream. Past a pond the path runs through colourful undergrowth, becoming enclosed to emerge at a house, Fox Covert. Its short

CONSTABLE BURTON • WALK 6

drive leads out onto No Man's Moor Lane, and crossing straight over, a path shadows telegraph poles across an open field. Joining a firm track, bear left over a gentle brow to reveal Finghall just ahead. Passing a massive shed, its firm access road runs on to drop to Blew House Lane on the village edge. Go left to the central junction, with the Queens Head pub in front: the walk returns to this point.

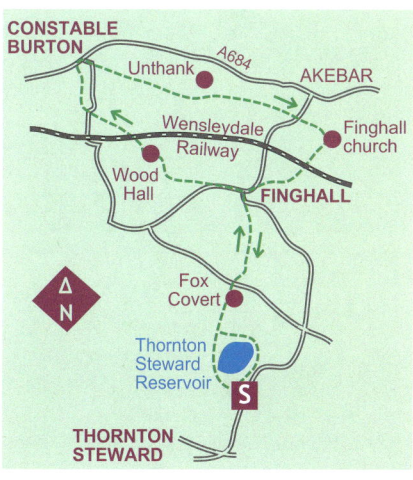

Finghall is a small, attractive street village perched on an elevated ridge. Just short of the junction is a minute old Wesleyan Chapel of 1845, while on the main street is its 1909 brick replacement. Finghall had its station on the Northallerton & Hawes Branch of the North Eastern Railway, and the station buildings survive down the lane. The track survived into the 1990s thanks to military use, and after a massive effort by its supporters, re-opened as the Wensleydale Railway in 2003. So Finghall's station exists again, currently the sole village station on the 17 miles from Leeming Bar to Redmire, the towns of Bedale and Leyburn providing the other stations.

Turn left on the road out of the village, and as it swings left keep on through a bridle-gate ahead. A hedgeside path heads away to a bridle-gate at the end. While the true line slants down to the right of the large barns of Wood Hall, a permissive route goes briefly left along the edge to turn down a better grassy way to an outer hedge corner, with the bend of a firm track just below. *An awkward five minutes in Croft Wood just ahead might be avoided by this locally used option: Turn right down the track (bridleway) to cross the railway, and at a bend just below, a grassy track (not a right of way) runs left across the field top to meet the footpath from Croft Wood below the railway crossing at the wood corner.*

WALK 6 • CONSTABLE BURTON

For the right of way to Croft Wood, go left past the barns, at the end turning right down a rough road behind an intriguing old barn. Approaching houses at Wood Hall below, don't swing right to them but take a thin path left into Croft Wood. It slants briefly down before quickly running left, enduring an uncomfortable five minutes amid brambles and fallen trees. Before long, locate a fainter branch dropping right through an appreciable gap for 50 yards to the railway line. Cross to find a cart track curving left back into trees, declining gently then along to the far bottom corner of the wood. A couple of gates send you across a small field to join a minor road. *This was Constable Burton's link with its station.*

Go left 30 yards to a stile in the wall on the right. Bear right to stiles at a plank bridge in the facing hedge, then turn right to a footbridge/ford on Sun Beck just below. Remain with the hedge on your right, up through a gate and over a slight brow to a bridle-gate overlooking Constable Burton. Bear slightly left down the field to a gate between gardens onto the A684. *Constable Burton is a tiny village south of the main road, while to the north stands Constable Burton Hall. Completed in 1768 by renowned architect John Carr of York, it is home to the Wyvills, one of the oldest families in the county: its beautiful gardens are open Friday to Sunday, April to June. The Wyvill Arms is a little further west along the road.* Yards to the right, turn along a side road above the green. *On your right are an old reading room and former school, while the sloping green falls to the beck and has a fine carved war memorial.* Swinging round the corner turn left on Mill Lane, losing its surface at an old chapel, with imposing Mill House in a lovely beckside setting below.

CONSTABLE BURTON • WALK 6

Continue along the cart track's pleasant course above wooded Burton Beck. At a fork stay on the lower option, through a gate. The track quickly ends at a tiny sewage works. Here begins the finest section of the walk, a delectable stroll on a slender green pasture with the beck alongside. A kissing-gate into trees deflects you from the beck, soon emerging into a field after a footbridge and bridle-gate. Keep left along the wooded edge, then a hedge is followed to the right-hand of two gates at the far end. Entering a lush beckside pasture, advance enjoyably on to a kissing-gate into a modest wooded bank at the far end - by now the stream is named Leeming Beck. Quickly taking a stile back into a field, cross to the right of Leeming Beck Bridge, with a bridle-gate onto a road.

Cross straight over and along the drive to Finghall church. *With its double bell-cote, St Andrew's little church stands in curious isolation, though over the wall is a large holiday park with a pub at Akebar.* Rise up the near side of the churchyard to a gate, and emerging into a sloping pasture, bear right up the near side of a streamlet. Entering a wooded gill, slant to a kissing-gate above to resume outside it. Rise to re-cross the railway, and in the field above bear right up to a corner kissing-gate. A short-lived green way runs to a kissing-gate onto Church Lane, continuing along it to Finghall. Advance to the junction and return as you came. From the bridle-gate into the reservoir grounds, vary the finish by swinging left around the knoll above the gorse slopes, and on through some scattered trees down to a waterworks road. Cross the curved dam and turn right to run above the shore back to the car park.

Opposite: Burton Beck *Finghall*

WALK 7 CRAKEHALL

A near-level stroll to a delightful village

START *Bedale (SE 265883; DL8 1EQ)*

DISTANCE *5½ miles (9km)*

ORDNANCE SURVEY 1:25,000 MAP
Explorer 302 - Northallerton & Thirsk

ACCESS *Start from the market place, various parking. Buses from Masham, Northallerton, Leyburn*

Bedale is a typical North Yorkshire market town with its Market Place being a broad main street with shops, pubs and cafes set back. St Gregory's church is a splendid building, fortified against Scots raids and containing fine effigies and wall paintings. In attractive gardens by Bedale Beck is the red-brick, castellated Leech House, a unique survivor from when live leeches were kept for medical purposes until needed to be used on patients! The early 18th century Bedale Hall includes a museum and tourist information. Bedale has a station on the Wensleydale Railway.

From Market Place head north towards the church. Immediately after Bedale Hall on the left, a surfaced path runs parallel to the road along the edge of playing fields. Soon reaching the end, you rejoin the road alongside the golf club. Ignore the road and go straight ahead along a sidelined section of old road. *This short length of the A684 was by-passed after construction of a link road to the upgraded A1(M) in 2016.* Merging into the A684, go left on the footway for 50 yards, then cross to a small patch of scrub: an initially unclear path heads away at an angle alongside a low hedge that quickly forms on your right. This leads to Bedale Sports Club, where you go straight ahead along the edge to a corner bridle-gate into an arable field. Crossing a track, a good path heads directly away to meet the railway line at the other side.

Don't cross but go left beneath it, through an intervening stile and along to meet a grassy track at the end: you shall return to this point to finish. Now turn right over the level crossing, and through a gate a grassy woodside track heads away. Crossing a stream a delectable hedgerowed way heads away, soon emerging to resume with a hedge on your right. Reaching a facing hedge at the end, turn right with it the short way to a gate onto a minor road at Kirkbridge. Turn right around the bend and on over a bridge on Bedale Beck. Just a little further you cross Kirk Bridge. *Rebuilt in 1958, an old tablet to the right dates from the original 1815 construction.* On leaving the hamlet, the road quickly arrives at an old milestone. *Dated 1795, it is inscribed with the destinations of Bedale, Catterick and Richmond.*

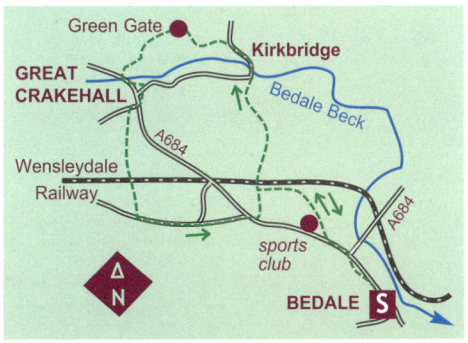

Opposite it, a gate set back on the left sends a grassy way off alongside a hedge, initially with the beck on your left. Reaching a recess on the right, a gate in it sends a cart track away with a hedge towards Green Gate Farm. It swings left to enter the yard, where go straight ahead and out on the access road, Green Gate Lane. Part way along, alongside a hut, a gate on the left sends a path across a small field centre to a kissing-gate, then runs enclosed to the right. Through a bridle-gate at the end it drops down to a parking area at Crakehall Watermill. *Dating back to the 17th century, it was initially restored in the 1970s and produces*

WALK 7 • CRAKEHALL

flour that is sold locally: it opens to visitors on the first Sunday of the month, April-October. Go straight across to drop down briefly enclosed, over a mill-cut to rejoin the beck alongside an intriguing arched boundary 'bridge'. A lovely path runs right with the beck onto a green to join the A684 in Crakehall, with a millpond to the right. Cross the road to find a footbridge over the beck, avoiding the triple-arched road bridge. Across, go left up into the centre.

Crakehall (strictly Great Crakehall) is dominated by a splendid spacious green. Ideally, re-cross and make a loop around it, with the benefit of a closer view of the imposing 18th century Crakehall Hall at the other side. *Also on the green are St Gregory's church with its 6-bell bell-cote, and a quoits pitch. Other amenities are the Bay Horse pub and a filling station with general store.* Further along, re-cross the main road at an angled crossroads and head away on the Burrill road past a small green. *You pass between an old Methodist church and a nice old chapel of 1840.* Immediately after the last house, take a gate/gap on the left into the first of a string of sheep pastures. Head away along a hedgeside to the same, then on to another. In the third field the path bears slightly right to a stile in a corner, then resumes with a hedge on your left. Through a gate ahead a brief enclosed section runs past an isolated house, emerging at a gate to resume with a hedge. At the end is a gate into a wooded corner, with stiles either side of the railway.

Resuming, part way along the next field a thin trod bears right to a stile by a lone tree onto a road. Go left for a long half-mile, over a crossroads and along to a junction with the A684. Cross to a footway and go very briefly right to bridge a drain just before a milestone. Whilst you could take the roadside footway back, nicer to turn left on a fieldside cart track to return to the corner by the level crossing. Turn right here to retrace opening steps.

The Leech House, Bedale

THORNBOROUGH HENGES

WALK 8

Easy walking and navigation encircling famous earthworks

START *Nosterfield (SE 278795; DL8 2QZ)*

DISTANCE *6¼ miles (10km)*

ORDNANCE SURVEY 1:25,000 MAP *Explorer 299 - Ripon & Boroughbridge & 302 - Northallerton & Thirsk*

ACCESS *Start from Nosterfield Nature Reserve car park on Moor Lane ¾-mile south of village: same distance from A6108, West Tanfield*

On the site of old quarries, Nosterfield Nature Reserve has lakes, reedbeds and rare grassland in a magnesian limestone habitat. An interpretation building and bird-hide overlook the main lake. Rejoining the road, turn left for a short stroll to a junction with the Nosterfield road. Turn right on a hedgerowed cart track (Green Lane) which runs a pleasant direct course, narrowing to a better path. Over to the left is the central, most prominent of the Thornborough Henges. Joining a road at the end, it is again well seen. *The henges comprise an aligned threesome of circular earthworks forming one of Britain's finest prehistoric sites. Dating back perhaps 5000 years to Neolithic times, each is some 790ft in diameter. In 2023 the site came into the care of English Heritage, with anticipated improved public access. Hitherto there had been no formal access to the henges, though this central one had the easiest unofficial access via a grassy hedgeside path from a gate on the left: look out for signs!*

WALK 8 • THORNBOROUGH HENGES

Back on the road, go briefly left to an easily-missed bridle-gate set back in a hedge-gap on the right. This sends a grassy little path directly away along a low bank, initially through pleasant pasture. Beyond a bridle-gate at a fence-end it continues straight on a large arable field, with the southern henge prominent just to your left. Through a gap in the strip plantation ahead, a cart track runs on with the strip to emerge onto a minor road. Go briefly left on the broad verge, and at Woodside House (Manor Farm Cottages on map), go left in front of it. Quickly emerging into a field corner, an excellent broad green path (another Green Lane) heads away with trees on your right. *Over to the left the southernmost henge is again well seen.* Its pleasant course even features a slight gradient as it runs to a gate, by which time the trees have ended. Here a firmer track merges from the right, and runs an unfailing, largely straight three-quarter mile course to ultimately join a road.

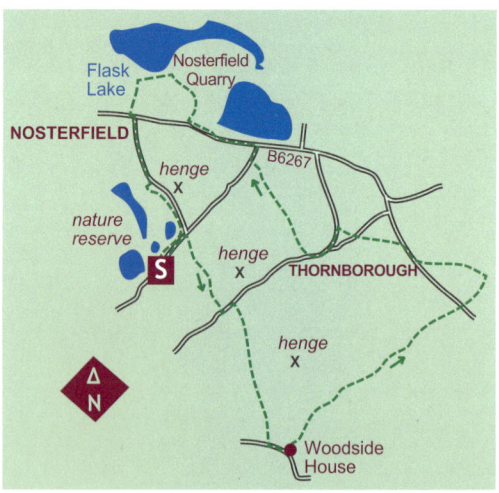

Cross and resume as before on a gentle rise to a brow. Dropping briefly away, when the hedge on your right turns off, take a clear path doubling back left across an arable field back to the brow. Through the old hedge-line the path continues on a gentle slant down a second field to a hedge-gap back onto the road. Go

THORNBOROUGH HENGES • WALK 8

briefly right, then at a field corner, take a gap just before the hedge on the left ends. This sends a direct path diagonally across another arable field to a corner stile onto a minor road. From one opposite, cross a narrow pasture to the right of modern barns, and a corner stile puts you onto a road-end in Thornborough. *This tiny village once had two Methodist chapels and the Hare & Hounds pub.* Go left along the street to rejoin the previous road, and advance a short way to the village edge. Just beyond the village sign, an enclosed old way turns right, soon emerging into an open field to run a splendid grassy course to emerge back onto Moor Lane. Go very briefly right to the B6267, then go left.

At the entrance to the active Nosterfield Quarry, enter and go left into a car park. A kissing-gate sends an enclosed permissive path away parallel with the road. At the end it turns right to resume pleasantly along to a corner with a quarry lake view. Turning left, it runs to join grassy Flask Lane. *A left turn would lead directly to Nosterfield.* Through a gap opposite, a path runs left parallel with the lane, through trees with Flask Lake to your right. Just 50 yards short of rejoining the now firmer lane at the end, a clear path turns sharp right to remain in trees. This runs on to a corner viewpoint overlooking the lake. At this path junction go a few yards left and take a stile into a sheep pasture on your left. Head diagonally away, over an intervening stile to reach a corner stile. With Nosterfield just ahead, cross to a small gate to follow a fenced course away past new housing to a stile back onto the B6267 in the village. Cross to the pub and go a few yards left to a junction by the green.

Surrounded by active and abandoned quarries, Nosterfield features the Freemasons Arms and a former Wesleyan chapel by a tiny green. Turn right along a side road out. *Where a path goes left by the village sign, you have a view of the tree-clad, northernmost of the henges, which came up for sale in 2023.* Just beyond the de-restriction sign, a kissing-gate on the right puts you back into Nosterfield Nature Reserve. *The right-hand path is a short cul-de-sac to a viewing screen for North Lake.* Going left, a firm, enclosed path runs a fieldside course parallel with the road. Entering trees and scrub it runs a pleasant course back to the car park above lakes on former silt lagoons. *You could explore further by taking a path running past the hide that invites further exploration.*

WALK 9
SNAPE PARK & WELL

Two historic villages linked by open fields and woodland

START *Snape (SE 266843; DL8 2TB)*

DISTANCE *6¼ miles (10km)*

ORDNANCE SURVEY 1:25,000 MAP
Explorer 302 - Northallerton & Thirsk

ACCESS *Start from the village centre, roadside parking. Masham-Bedale bus.*

Snape is a splendid street village best known for its castle, stood in isolation at the western end. Built as a manor house in the first half of the 15th century, the great hall and chapel are the best surviving features. Catherine Parr, surviving wife of Henry VIII, lived here while married to John Neville. The great house underwent periods of neglect until acquired by William Milbank of nearby Thorpe Perrow in 1798. Though in private hands, it is well seen from the road and the chapel approach. An integral part of the main building, the impressive St Mary's chapel still serves the parish of Well with Snape, and can be visited by a path along the edge of the adjacent yard. Focal point of village life is the Castle Arms, with a high quality grocery store nearby. The game of quoits is played here, one of numerous local activities to feature on the Millennium Stone on the village green. This extends a considerable length of the village and a stream runs through: two village pumps still stand, as does a memorial of 1874 to Lady Augusta Milbank.

SNAPE PARK & WELL • WALK 9

Head east along the main street and out on the Carthorpe road. The houses end at once, and a couple of minutes further a stile is reached on the right, with a benchmark on the old gatepost. Head away along the fenceside, and at the far end a footbridge puts you in the next field. Advance to the end and bear left along the top side. Reaching an outer corner, turn through the large gap and resume with the hedge on your left, now on a good path. Towards the end it bears left to a stile set slightly back.

With a tall hedge to your left, head away along a lush sheep pasture that slowly tapers to a stile at the end. Now follow the right edge of a field a short way, then pass through a gap on a farm bridge on Low Park Beck. Just 50 yards along the cart track heading away, take a thin, clear path heading into a corner of Low Park Wood. Quickly joined by another path from the right, it runs a delightful course to emerge into a large field. The village of Well awaits, just ahead now.

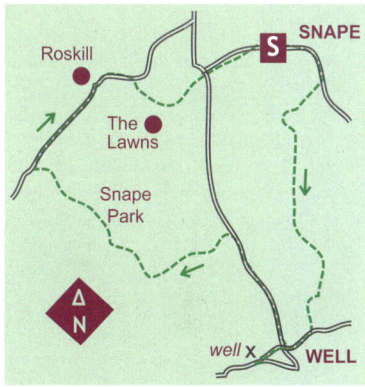

Advance to the corner just ahead, noting a reedy pond to your left. Here the right of way rises gently up the field centre, keeping to the right of a line of telegraph poles and aiming left of the church. It may be easier to follow a broad way rising directly up, passing through the poles to reach a hedge at the top. A path runs right with it to a pole at an outer corner by an emerging drain. From the inner corner just behind, an enclosed path runs alongside the channel, quickly swinging right and along to a fork in front of an industrial yard. From a kissing-gate on the left, a snicket runs by the churchyard out onto Church Street in Well.

Turn right to the staggered crossroads by the Milbank Arms. *Well is an attractive village sheltering beneath its steep bank. Along the way you pass the church, 18th century almshouses and Well Hall. St Michael's is a lovely old church containing the impressive John Neville tomb. Evidence of a Roman bath-house has*

WALK 9 • SNAPE PARK & WELL

been discovered here. While your route is right, first consider a visit to St Michael's Well. Head away along the side road ahead, past a former chapel of 1849 and up a short little pull leading to the de-restriction sign. With a pond and lodge on the right, just 75 yards further, at your feet on the right is St Michael's Well. Here clear water appears and runs into the beck.

Leave by heading along Bedale Road from the pub, which is followed out of the village for around ten minutes. On reaching a distinctive belt of trees, turn up a good fieldside track on its near side. At the field top this turns into the shelter of the trees. Don't re-emerge at the other side however, but take a clear path rising left up the centre of the wood known as The Belt. Through a carpet of springtime wild garlic, this ascends delightfully and unfailingly for a considerable time, easing out before finally swinging right to a gateway. Follow the right side of a hedge away to the corner of Grays Plantation ahead. *The slope of the old deer park of Snape Park beneath you affords views over the Vale of Mowbray, with the landmark of Roseberry Topping discerned at the northern limit of the Cleveland Hills.*

A good little path runs along the wood top, and emerging at a bridle-gate, descend to another by a pond to join a drive. From a

SNAPE PARK & WELL • WALK 9

stile almost opposite, ascend a hedgeside with the house of Snape Park to the left (not quite as per map). Through an intervening gate continue to a stile at the end, and after just a few yards of undergrowth, cross a track to resume with a hedge on your right. This rises gently alongside a massive field to the walk's high point at 375ft/115m, and all the way on past the wood at Warrener's Bottom to swing round at the end onto a back road, Moor Lane. *Seen up the slope just ahead is a distinctive 17th century dovecote at Watlass Moor House.*

Turn right to commence a gentle three-quarter mile descent, largely with broad verges. *Massive views again look east to the eternal escarpments of the North York Moors.* A little past Roskill Farm, now level, a gateway on the right just before a bend left sends a hedgeside cart track away to a belt of woodland. Through the slender gap it runs on to quickly join the drive to The Lawns (Snape Lawns on map), just to your right. Turn left on this, over a brow and down to a crossroads. Cross straight over to re-enter Snape, making use of broad and colourful verges beneath an avenue of limes, before a footway leads past the castle.

Opposite: Snape Castle   *The Castle Arms, Snape*

WALK 10
AROUND PICKHILL

Easy rambling in an unfrequented backwater

START Sinderby (SE 345819; YO7 4JD)

DISTANCE 7 miles (11¼km) (with shorter option)

ORDNANCE SURVEY 1:25,000 MAP
Explorer 302 - Northallerton & Thirsk

ACCESS Start from the village centre, roadside parking.

Sinderby is a tiny, very peaceful village set around a sizeable green. A former Methodist Chapel now serves as a village hall. Sinderby's station on the railway from Ripon to Northallerton closed in 1962, some five years before the line itself. Leave by the Pickhill road passing the village hall, and virtually at once meeting a junction. Take the side road right for around half a mile to a junction just before Holme. Keep left the short way to within yards of the hamlet entrance, then go left on a rough access road. *This is Church Lane, the old churchgoers' route to Pickhill for residents of Holme.*

When it turns off left to a farm at Holme Lodge, advance straight on a nicer hedgerowed cart track: the aforementioned church appears ahead. When this ends at an arable field, advance on a green way along the edge with a new hedge as far as a gate in it at a small kink. Through it bear right to resume with a hedge

AROUND PICKHILL • WALK 10

on your right, commencing a near-straight line through cushioned pastures to Pickhill. Through a gate at the end, cross a field centre to another corner gate where a hedge rejoins. A final long pasture leads to Pickhill, where a pair of gates alongside the school put you onto a rough lane in the village, with the green just to your left. You shall return here after the Swainby loop.

Pickhill's houses line a street that emerges onto the focal point of a spacious green. Set on a distinct knoll, All Saints church has a 15th century tower and a carved Norman doorway: inside is a 10th century Viking hog-back carving. Along the street are a former Wesleyan Chapel of 1864 and also the Nags Head pub. Pickhill also had its own rail station until closure in 1959. Note that the loop can be omitted (halving the mileage) by crossing the green onto the through road and turning left.

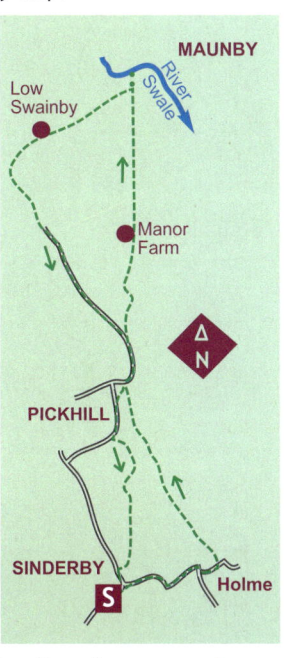

Resume on the road on your side, and keep straight on at the end beneath the church. After Church Farm it swings left through an old rail embankment gap. Just after a track rises onto the line, take a stile in the hedge to the right. Head away along a field parallel with the old line's low cutting on your right. *The Hambleton Hills are well seen over to the right.*

A stile at the end puts you onto a junction of access roads near Highfield Farm: take the nicer track left the short way to meet a like track. Go right towards a house at Landends, but quickly take a stile on the left. Head away across an enclosure outside some outbuildings to a stile at the end. Advance with a hedge on your left to a stile just short of the end. Entering a tiny wooded corner, bear right to a kissing-gate into a field. Head away with a row of tree plantings towards Manor Farm, keeping right of its confines to a gate at the end alongside a holiday cottage and old farmyard.

WALK 10 • AROUND PICKHILL

Whilst a cart track drops down onto the old railway, for now remain on the public footpath through a kissing-gate ahead, to again run parallel to the old line. On through another stile, a tiny branch track comes up from the railway track into the next field. Due to an impasse ahead, at this point it is advisable to transfer to the track: though not a right of way, it is the preferred (and in truth only) local option. *For the record, the right of way takes a kissing-gate in front and on to another into an arable field. The lack of a path underfoot is more crucially compounded by the exit at the end being entirely impassable. Were you able to pass through, you would then advance on the left edge of the wedge of trees here, emerging to trace a hedge on your left to its demise, then continuing to trample crops along to an access road.*

Joining the track at this point, it leads splendidly along to drop to a junction at the end. While the onward route is the firm access road left, it is interesting to first go right the very short way (now a cart track) to Maunby rail bridge on the meandering River Swale. *Whilst not a public right of way, the landowners on either side permit access across it. One side of the iron bridge is adorned with an appropriately styled range of admirable quotations. A ferry once operated here just a few yards upstream, where a bridleway is marked as fording the river. Across the bridge a hedgerowed cart track runs to an access road on the edge of Maunby village, though sadly its Buck Inn closed in only recent times.*

AROUND PICKHILL • WALK 10

Back at the junction head away on the access road, passing Swale House to reach Low Swainby Farm with a fine red-brick house. Continue along the parkland drive to emerge at a junction with Swainby Lane, here just a bridleway. *Back over to your right is the site of a substantial medieval settlement that grew around the Premonstratensian Swainby Abbey, though the actual abbey community moved to Coverham, near Middleham in the early 13th century, leaving just a grange here.* Go left for a pleasant stroll with some decent verges, the fully surfaced bridleway later becoming a public road. Its hedgerowed course runs on to absorb your outward route on the edge of Pickhill.

Back on the green, bear right at the end along the main street past the pub. As the road swings right, double back left on an access road towards a farmyard. Quickly take a gate on the left outside a house, and on to enter a field. Go right to the furthest gate on the right just short of the corner, and head away with a hedge on your left. Through a gateway in it just before the end, advance on with a hedge on your right. Part way on, a stile sends you through a belt of trees into an arable field. An excellent path runs along the left edge to a rough track at the far corner of a modern barn cluster. Across it your path resumes to a stile at the end. Go briefly right to a gate sending a hedgerowed green way the short way out onto a road, and go left to re-enter the village.

Maunby rail bridge on the Swale

Opposite: Sinderby

WALK 11: COD BECK & SOWERBY

An unsung stream is key to a wealth of interest both in and around an absorbing market town

START Thirsk (SE 429820; YO7 1EY)

DISTANCE 5¾ miles (9¼km)

ORDNANCE SURVEY 1:25,000 MAP
Explorer 302 - Northallerton & Thirsk

ACCESS Start from the market place, car parks.
Bus from Northallerton, Ripon, York, and railway station.

Thirsk is a splendid, bustling town based around an extensive market place, market days being Monday and Saturday. Pubs, cafes and independent shops fan out beyond the market place, which has an information centre near Thirsk's iconic clock tower of 1896. Also within and beyond the market place is a wealth of interesting buildings, while Cod Beck glides innocuously around the back. The World of James Herriot pays tribute to the world famous vet Alf Wight, whose adventures in print have also been immortalized on both film and television: the museum occupies the original surgery. Across the street is the lesser-known Thirsk Museum. St Mary's church dates from the 15th century and boasts a hugely impressive frontage: alongside is Thirsk Hall, dating from 1723 and home to a sculpture garden. Last but not least, Thirsk boasts one of Yorkshire's many celebrated racecourses.

From the clock tower go east the short way to the main road's corner exit along Millgate. Quickly approaching triple-arched Mill Bridge on Cod Beck, instead cross the side road of Marage Road onto a surfaced path that runs through a picnic area to a footbridge on the beck. Across, double back left to a gate into a recreation area, and cross to a kissing-gate at the far end. A clear path heads away through undergrowth, through another kissing-gate and on through trees to a footbridge on the beck at a weir. Don't cross but resume on the path ahead through further unkempt grassland, ignoring a branch right.

On opening out a little more on your right, the somewhat thinner path continues as before until reaching a farm bridge. Again ignore, and advance on a clear little path across a large open pasture, short-cutting the beck's meanderings. Reaching a ford on the beck at the far end, ignore stiles either side and turn briefly right to a corner kissing-gate, with a stile behind it into a field. A faint path swings left with the beck to a stile, and on to one into a few trees. The now enclosed path commences a super stroll tight by the beck, along the backs of the gardens of South Kilvington and ultimately

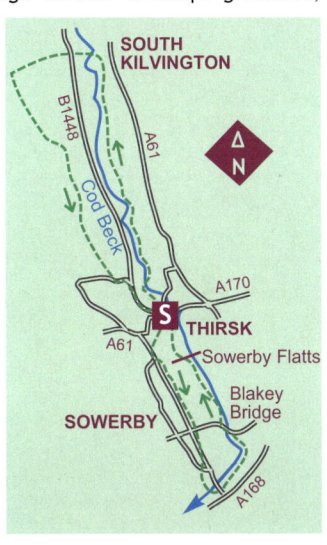

with a mill-cut the short way to emerge in front of the old mill. *This impressive former cornmill occupies a lovely spot, and with a waterwheel still in place the owner still operates it on occasions. Just to your right the village is set along the A61 (the old A19), with the Old Oak Tree pub and St Wilfrid's attractive little church.*

Cross the footbridge on your left over the cut, and a path bears right past its grounds to a broader bridge on Cod Beck itself. *At the time of research this was being dismantled, with a replacement hopefully in place during 2024. If not, you'd have to advance along the village road to a roundabout, go left on the A168 then double*

WALK 11 • COD BECK & SOWERBY

back left on the B1448. Across, head away to a bridle-gate onto an old section of road by the B1448. From a gap/gate opposite, a broad grassy way rises between arable fields to level out at a gateway. *Look back to appraise the long line of the Hambleton Hills.* The improving cart track runs on outside Underwood Plantation. *Levelling out, the hills of the Yorkshire Dales appear, dominated by shapely Penhill: Dales and Moors now take turns to feature in views.* The track runs on to a crossroads of such ways at a hedge.

Take the grassy hedgeside track sharp left along an arable fieldside. Through a hedge it continues to a kissing-gate in your hedge, from where the path runs diagonally across a pasture to a kissing-gate at the far corner. A continuing path crosses the centre of an arable field, bearing slightly left to a corner hedge-gap. A path resumes with a hedge on your left, then on through a broad hedge-gap to an enclosed section known as Wetlands Lane. This runs grandly on for some time to reach modern housing. Advance straight on the grassy way, becoming a cart track between gardens, allotments and then cemetery to emerge onto a road. Go left on this to re-enter town alongside the church, and go right past Thirsk Hall and along Kirkgate to re-enter the market place.

For the second, shorter part, cross to the south side and take an alley (Roses Yard) between shops just right of the Three Tuns. This runs out as a cobbled lane onto Chapel Street, which cross straight over to a snicket at Villa Place between houses. Emerging into a grassy sward alongside the leisure centre, remain on the surfaced path bearing right past a playground to emerge by a road on the edge of Sowerby. Go left on the footway which has a spell away from the road before rejoining it to reach the church. *St Oswald's features a fine Norman doorway this side of the porch.*

COD BECK & SOWERBY • WALK 11

Resuming, a broad, linear green keeps the road at bay for some time. *This hugely attractive Georgian street includes half-timbered Oxmoor Farm and the Crown & Anchor pub.* When the green finally ends, advance on the footway to a smaller green at the village edge, with the Thirsk by-pass just ahead. Bear right on a footway to meet Back Lane, just back from the junction, and cross to a side road opposite. After 50 yards bear left at Worlds End (a former pub), becoming a short, hedgerowed path to arrive at Town End Bridge. *This splendid packhorse bridge dates from the 17th century.* Across, advance to the road ahead and cross to a kissing-gate into open pasture. A good path bears left to run close by Cod Beck, through a kissing-gate and on to pass Pudding Pie Hill. *This distinct little mound is a 4000-year old Bronze Age burial site.*

Just a little further, the path emerges onto Blakey Lane at Blakey Bridge. Across it resume upstream, quickly becoming enclosed to run a nice beckside course to stone-arched Lock Bridge. *In 1763 the canal boom saw plans to make the beck navigable for some seven miles from its confluence with the Swale near Topcliffe. A lock was planned here, and work had already started on the basin upstream before financial issues saw the scheme abandoned. The beck flows briefly widely at this pleasant spot.* Don't cross but resume on a broad, grassy path bearing gently away from the beck across Sowerby Flatts. At a fork keep right to run to a kissing-gate, then along to the leisure centre to finish as you began.

Opposite: Kilvington Mill   *Cod Beck at Sowerby Flatts*

WALK 12: AROUND FELIXKIRK

Richly varied paths link lovely villages in colourful country

START Boltby (SE 492866; YO7 2DY)

DISTANCE 7¼ miles (11½km)

ORDNANCE SURVEY 1:25,000 MAP
Explorer OL26 - North York Moors West

ACCESS Start from the village centre, roadside parking. Also parking areas on road south (on route), and above east end. Note that a section between Kirby Knowle and Carr Hill can become hampered by nettles/brambles in summer months.

Boltby is an immensely attractive village in the shadow of the Hambleton Hills. With tidy stone cottages under red pantile roofs, its enviable setting renders it near perfect. The modest church of the Holy Trinity sports a small bell-cote, and there is a trekking centre nearby. Head west along the street from the church, out of the village and ignoring a left branch to rise to a brow. After the second drive right (West Acre Lodge), it starts to descend: look out for a bridle-gate set back in the hedge on your right. Entering a sloping pasture, head directly away at mid-height, merging with the fence below further on to cross a stile in it before reaching a wood.

Above a hawthorn bank bear right, slanting down to the shallow valley floor and along to a stile at the end. Now advance on with trees and fence on your right, a little path forming in this broad

AROUND FELIXKIRK • WALK 12

hollow. When fence and trees turn off, keep straight on the open grassy trough. With the colourful, steep wooded slopes of Birk Bank above, bear gently right to a corner where a simple footbridge crosses a drain to resume as before. Maintain this line beneath the bank to a stile at the end. Drop left a few yards to escape the bracken, and slant down onto a grassy track heading along the trough. Firming up and entering trees at the end, a junction is quickly reached. From a bridle-gate on the left drop down a field-side with a fence on your right, through a gate at the bottom and across to a hedge corner. Just past it is a kissing-gate onto a road in the hamlet of Kirby Knowle, across from the old school.

A couple of yards left is a junction with the through road, where go left past the 19th century church of St Wilfred. Keep straight on at a grassy triangle junction, and leaving the hamlet it's a short stroll to reach a stile set back in a hedge on the left. *Ahead up to the right is a grand house on the site of the 13th century Kirby Knowle Castle, much restored in modern times.*

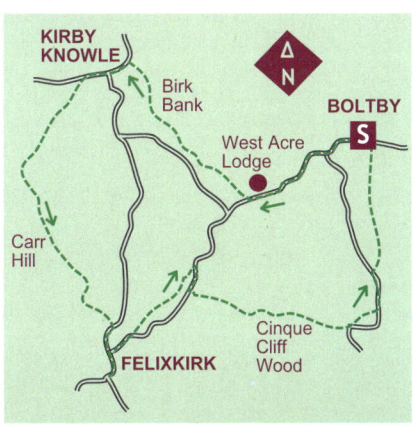

Head away close by a wooded streamlet on your left, a track forming to run to some gates. From a stile by the left-hand one an enclosed path runs between stream and fence, a course maintained for some time. The path intermittently opens out into fieldsides, and later improves when closer to the stream. Ultimately you arrive at a sidestream.

Just yards after crossing the sidestream you emerge into an arable field corner. Advance less than 20 yards left along the edge to locate your onward path delving into trees and scrub to cross the short way back to finally arrive alongside Beechpath Beck. Across a rudimentary bridge, a path rises into an arable field bottom, and up its tree-lined left side. For some time now simply continue with

WALK 12 • AROUND FELIXKIRK

the field boundary on your left and along the brow of Carr Hill. *Big views look west across the vale to the hills of the Yorkshire Dales.* At the end a little path delves briefly left into the unkempt corner, then emerges to resume as before. Keep on to a stile/gate, and on to another gate. Ignoring a stile/plank bridge on your left, drop a little at the end to a stile/gate into trees. Crossing tiny Nevison Beck, up the other bank you emerge into colourful pasture. *On your left is the ditch of Paled Dike, an ancient deer park boundary.*

Rise very gently right across the brow and cross to a stile and plank bridge on a streamlet. A rough path runs left through scrub along a field edge to soon reach a bridle-gate into a more welcoming field. Go left with the hedge, using a bridle-gate in it near the end to follow the other side the short way to a gate onto a road. Go briefly right to a junction on the edge of Felixkirk, and while your onward route is left, first advance for just one minute into the tiny village. *St Felix's church dates from the 12th century, and contains fine effigies of a knight and his wife. The Carpenters Arms sits opposite the distinctive ancient knoll of Howe Hill, while alongside is the old school. Mount St John overlooking the village was the site of a preceptory of the Knights Hospitallers of St John.*

Back on the road out, keep right on the Boltby road as it rises gently away. At a slight bend a little higher, a stile on the left sends an invisible path across a colourful, sloping bank. *Adorned in spring-*

AROUND FELIXKIRK • WALK 12

time with hawthorn blossom, this enjoys lovely views. Beyond an early stile maintain your course, rising slightly after a messy few yards beneath gorse, and aiming for a gate in a fence ahead. Through it a grassy track forms to rise to a stile/gate in front of a wood. Double back right along the road a short way, still looking over the bank. Where an unsigned back road goes left at a cattle-grid/gate, follow it away into open surrounds. *Ahead, the skyline of Boltby Scar soon leads all the way round to Whitestone Cliff and Roulston Scar.* Ignore branches right then left, passing alongside Cinque Cliff Wood before it drops down to the bend of a road.

Just yards before the road take a stile on the left, crossing a slim enclosure to a corner gate just ahead, then diagonally cross a larger sheep pasture to find a corner stile back onto the road. Go left until reaching a small lay-by just after a large one. Set back here is a bridle-gate, and a grassy path heads away with the field boundary and Girtof Beck on your right. This is maintained for some time, with Boltby appearing ahead. Seeing more of the beck and crossing two sidestreams, you arrive at a bridle-gate, where leave the beck to bear left across a field centre. Through an intervening fence-gate cross to another gate at the village edge, and on through two further gates to follow a short grassy track out with the stream, a delightful finish between a former Wesleyan chapel and a charming stone-arched little bridge.

Opposite: Felixkirk church  *Carpenters Arms, Felixkirk*

WALK 13 BORROWBY BANKS

Far-reaching views from slopes around a scenic hillside village

START *Knayton (SE 432880; YO7 4AZ)*

DISTANCE *6 miles (9½km)*

ORDNANCE SURVEY 1:25,000 MAP
Explorer 302 - Northallerton & Thirsk

ACCESS *Start from the village centre, roadside parking*

Knayton is a small village alongside the A19 with the Dog & Gun pub opposite a small green bearing the village hall. Facing the pub head left along the road to bridge the dual carriageway, and a tarmac path immediately drops right onto a section of old road, with a road (the old A19) just ahead. Advance on the footway past the school, quickly reaching a left fork at the edge of Borrowby. With a slight short-cut bear left, and very quickly, just after the 30mph sign, turn left on the unsigned firm track of Bob Lane. Past the sewage works it drops down to end at stables. From a stile/gate in front, a thin path drops right with the hedge, curving around to a small corner gate. A barely enclosed path heads away to reach a concrete slab bridging a streamlet, then heads away to a gate. It then runs more faintly on across a sheep pasture to reach a corner stile/gate onto Allerton Wath Road.

Go right a short way to a kink, and take a gate on the right. A slender path heads directly away between the arable crops to a

BORROWBY BANKS • WALK 13

hedge at the other side. Go left a short way to a metal kissing-gate in it, and a clear path rises gently away to a gate in the hedge at the top. Cross to a gate in a recess, then bear left more steeply up to a gate set back between houses. A short enclosed way rises into the centre of Borrowby, with a small Methodist chapel on your right. *This delightful village features a long, sloping street lined by attractive cottages, especially on its east side. A small, sloping green is straight ahead, bearing a splendid old market cross on tiered steps outside the village hall. At the crossroads just below is the homely Wheatsheaf pub. Borrowby Show is a popular local event in late July.*

Go left on the side road quickly leaving the village. Immediately after the last house as it drops away, take a gate on the right with another one just behind. *Throughout much of this walk extensive views look west over the Vale of Mowbray to the moors of the Yorkshire Dales, with Penhill prominent at the foot of Wensleydale.* A grassy track heads away, but quickly leave on a thinner forming path to the right, crossing the field centre to a corner gate in front of white-walled St Helen's Cottage. Joining the track of St Helen's Lane behind, turn left down its hedgerowed course. Emerging at a gate into a field, continue down

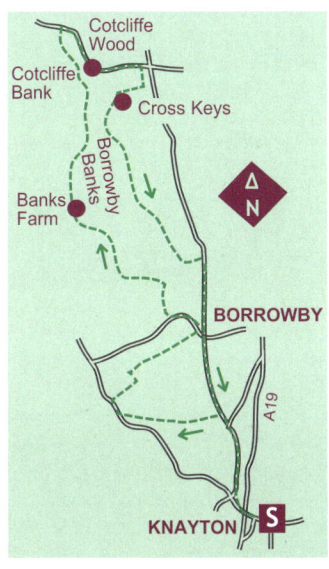

to a corner gate just below. Through it the track turns right along a field top, ending at a gate into an arable field. Continue along the hedgeside the short way to a gate into a sloping pasture. Drop briefly down to a footbridge/stile, then bear left over a minor brow and down to the buildings at Carrodale.

Pass between house and outbuildings to a gate where its drive heads away: instead take a stile on the right onto another drive. Cross to a bridle-gate opposite, and away along a field top outside

WALK 13 • BORROWBY BANKS

Banks Farm to a stile/gate at the far end. An old track forms to run above a small wooded bank to a stile/gate into a large sloping field. A little path heads away along Borrowby Banks, but as it fades slant right to a stile higher up the facing fence than the map suggests. Through a belt of trees to another stile, resume across a field beneath a wood to a gate, and beneath further trees to another.

Approaching Cotcliffe Bank Farm, a faint grassy way crosses a colourful pasture, and at the next gate (above the corner of a small wood), as a firmer track reaches outbuildings, instead take a gate left and slant down the bank to a stile in the bottom. Advance to a gate ahead, but use an adjacent stile and tiny, overgrown footbridge into the corner of a tall grass field. Head diagonally away aiming for buildings ahead. Through an old fence cross to a gate into a horse paddock, and on to a bridle-gate nearer the buildings. Now turn right along the fieldside to a stile onto a road, with stone-arched Cotcliffe Bridge on Cod Beck immediately to your left.

Your route is right, the road soon climbing Cotcliffe Bank beneath Cotcliffe Wood, passing Cotcliffe Bank Farm and up a wooded recess past quarried cliffs. Easing up on leaving the trees, take a gate on the right just before a junction. Follow a hedge away, staying with it when it turns right through a corner stile. This precedes a quick succession of stiles inside the grounds of the house at the former Cross Keys Farm. From the final stile into a narrow field, bear slightly left to a stile opposite, then cross to a hedge below and follow it left. Through an intervening gate advance on, and as the hedge turns off, cross to one ahead. Rise left with it the short way to a recess, and through the stile/gate on your right head away with a hedge along an arable fieldside.

Over a minor brow on Burtree Hills continue gently down to a corner, where a stile hides in the hedge on your left. Rise right up to an outer corner, and maintain this slant to a stile in the rising hedge opposite. Cross straight over a field to a hedge-gap opposite, then drop left to a corner stile/gate back onto St Helen's Lane. Go left on its short, hollowed way to emerge onto a road on the edge of Borrowby, and turn right down through the village. Intermittent grass verges on the left afford a break from the tarmac. *While Back Lane on the left offers an early variant, it is less attractive than the main street itself.* Back in the village centre, continue straight down to absorb your outward route back to Knayton.

AROUND THE SILTONS

WALK 14

Peaceful hamlets under the Hambleton escarpment

START *Thimbleby (SE 449953; DL6 3PY)*

DISTANCE *5¼ miles (8½km)*

ORDNANCE SURVEY 1:25,000 MAP
Explorer OL26 - North York Moors West

ACCESS *Start from the village centre, roadside parking*

Thimbleby is a tiny community along a small street that once featured a pub and a reading room. At the walk's start you pass Thimbleby Shooting Ground, which also features archery and a café. By the entrance is a splendid old bridle-road sign. Head south along the street to the village edge, past the shooting ground to a bend. Here a gate on the left sends the hedgerowed cart track of Jemmy Lane away to end with a slight rise left to a gate into a sloping sheep pasture. The diverted route here briefly differs slightly from older maps. Advance along the bottom with the hedge, and ignoring a gate at the end, turn up the near side of the fence to reach a bridle-gate in it. Through it head away on Creak Hill, and approaching a fence-gate, don't pass through but turn down its near side to a gate/bridle-gate at the bottom.

Entering a grassy trough beneath old jet workings, turn right along its floor on a path beneath a gorse bank. Soon opening out, the path fades. Bear left, but within a hundred yards, a little path

WALK 14 • AROUND THE SILTONS

doubles back left up an obvious break in the bank. This rapidly improves as it ascends, then swings right beneath a plantation to a bridle-gate into the trees. Joining a broad, level path just above, turn right for a splendid stroll largely along the wood bottom. *Passing above a farm, note the craggy wall of The Scar above you.* Delving back into trees comes an immediate fork: take the path slanting left, a briefly steep section putting you at the wood top. Go right, passing outbuildings to quickly reach a small gate into a garden. Advance briefly on, then left on the near side of the house to emerge on its drive running the short way out onto a lane in the hamlet of Over Silton.

Drop right past a tiny former school of 1844 onto the through road, then very briefly left to a junction. Turning down, look for an early stile in the hedge on the left beneath a telegraph pole. Entering rough pasture bear right, slanting away from the hedge to a stile in the bottom corner. Go left to a gate, then a little path drops to cross a stream. It then runs right, rising into the yard at Greystone Farm. Follow the drive out onto a road on the edge of Nether Silton, and go left past Silton Hall into the village. *Well off the beaten track, this small settlement features a large, sloping green with quoits pitch, the Gold Cup inn and the modest All Saints church.*

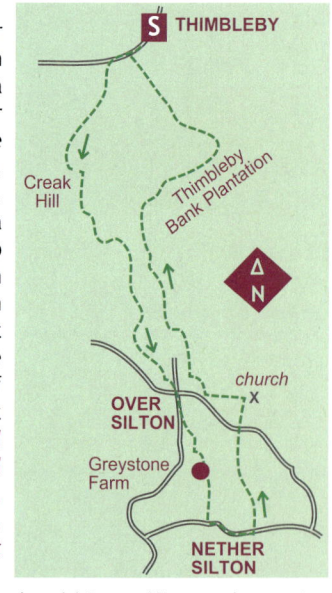

Advance just a short way past the old Post office, and opposite the churchyard corner a small gate on the left sends an enclosed path out to a stile into a field. Continuing as a hedgeside path, this runs a very pleasant, uncomplicated course along several fields linked by stiles. With Over Silton church appearing ahead, at the end you drop to a stile/gate onto Kirk Ings Lane. From a stile/gate set back opposite, a grassy track rises up a fieldside to St Mary's

AROUND THE SILTONS • WALK 14

church. *Couched in remarkable isolation amid lush pastures, it dates back to the 12th century and occasional services are still held from Easter Sunday through to Harvest Festival.* Leave by heading directly away from the gate, a path forming on the nick just ahead. This runs towards a gate/stile onto the road at the entrance back into Over Silton.

Note that you could advance a short way along the road then turn right up a rough access road to a plantation to meet the main route. However, without joining the road take a corner bridle-gate, then along a short fieldside to a gate ahead. Now go left on a concrete track, keeping right on it at the rear of a farmyard. Just a little further it turns left into another yard, but here take a stile in front. Continue in a straight line through successive stiles to rise into a plantation above. Go left on the forest road, dropping briefly past an old quarry to find a bridle-path rising to the right. Briefly climbing, it eases out to run nicely along the wood edge.

Joining an intermittently rutted but generally good forest road, advance along into the trees, dropping down before levelling to merge with a harder forest road from the left. Resume along this to reach a junction of ways. From a gate/bridle-gate on the left, leave the trees for the track of Sandpit Lane. With great views northwards to Osmotherley, it soon descends to emerge by the shooting ground on the edge of Thimbleby.

Over Silton church

WALK 15 SCARTH WOOD MOOR

Fantastic views from glorious heather moorland above an archetypal North York Moors village

START Osmotherley (SE 456972; DL6 3AA)

DISTANCE 6 miles (9½km)

ORDNANCE SURVEY 1:25,000 MAP
Explorer OL26 - North York Moors West

ACCESS Start from the village centre, roadside parking. Northallerton-Stokesley bus.

Osmotherley has a highly attractive village centre where a small green marks the meeting of roads lined by stone cottages, the main street sloping throughout its length. On the green is a sturdy market cross, next to which is a stone table where John Wesley once preached: just around the back is his early Methodist chapel of 1754. Almost everything is centrally placed, with the church of St Peter showing traces of Norman work, and three pubs. There are also tearooms, shop, chippy, youth hostel and an annual agricultural show. Starting point for the infamous Lyke Wake Walk, Osmotherley has a special 'ramblers' atmosphere.

Much of your outward route follows the Cleveland Way. Leave by the Swainby road (High Street) climbing north, passing a former chapel and former pinfold. When it eases, go left on the access road of Ruebury Lane, passing several houses to lose its surface. At

SCARTH WOOD MOOR • WALK 15

a fork just a little further, take the right branch signed to the Lady Chapel alongside a view indicator. This rises steadily and runs on through trees, with the Stations of the Cross appearing on your right at regular intervals. Before too long a few stone steps lead up to the chapel. *Dating from the 15th century but rebuilt in the mid 20th century, the shrine of Our Lady of Mount Grace still hosts Roman Catholic services in this very peaceful setting.*

At the far end of the site a broad path drops through a few trees to a bridle-gate back onto the Cleveland Way. Turn right for a grand stroll between scrub and a wall with massive views over the Vale of Mowbray to the Yorkshire Dales skyline. Through a bridle-gate at the end the path enters recent woodland, running on then slanting down to a bottom corner bridle-gate onto a path junction. A kissing-gate on the right puts you into South Wood. Meeting the Coast to Coast Walk here, take the path slanting right, a splendid 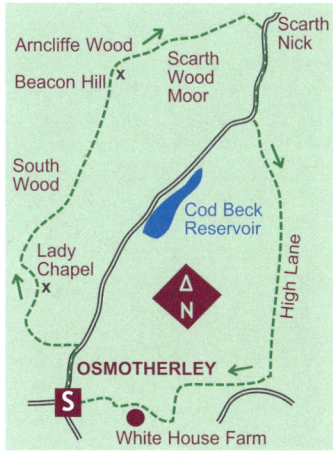 rise up the wood. After passing a viewpoint knoll, it rises more directly to reach the wood top. Now level, it runs left with a wall to emerge suddenly alongside the masts and paraphernalia of a long-established communications station.

Squeezing past the enclosure the path resumes along the top of Arncliffe Wood. *Views open out ahead to shapely Carlton Moor and around to the even shapelier if distant Roseberry Topping: an Ordnance Survey column at 981ft/299m on Beacon Hill hides just over the wall alongside you.* At the end the path drops a little to adjacent gates onto a corner of Scarth Wood Moor, a splendid moment. The path drops steadily down across the heart of the moor, encountering increasing heather to reach a fork just after a wall comes in. Leaving the Cleveland Way (for now), keep to the firmer right branch which slants down onto the Osmotherley-Swainby road above Scarth Nick.

WALK 15 • SCARTH WOOD MOOR

Turn right for a third of a mile, for the most part on verges or parallel path. At a sharp bend right towards a car park, take the rough road straight ahead down to a ford/footbridge at Sheepwash on Cod Beck. A brief climb of Sheep Wash Bank sends the old road (High Lane) on for a grand stride between dense swathes of heather with big views. Reaching a plantation corner the views diminish, but the firm track runs endlessly on for a further three-quarters of a miles above the trees. Generally gently rising, it becomes enclosed, often with an adjacent verge path until ultimately the trees end. *Revealed are massive views, notably ahead to the great prow of Black Hambleton.*

Finally level, you are joined by a farm road, soon becoming surfaced. When it prepares to drop to the Osmotherley-Hawnby road, instead turn right on a hugely inviting grassy track. This runs on a fenceside above bracken slopes with great views over wooded Oakdale to Black Hambleton. At the end, take a stile in front and continue along a wallside rough pasture. Through a gate at the end you earn a super view over the village and its environs, and the now enclosed grassy path drops onto a horse track. From a bridle-gate/stile behind, turn left on the enclosed path of Green Lane, soon dropping through greenery to level out at a cross-path. Through a gap-stile on the right you join a grassy access road, now back on the Cleveland Way to conclude.

SCARTH WOOD MOOR • WALK 15

Turn right, soon swinging left down towards White House Farm. Before it, your path contours right across a sloping pasture well above the farm. At the corner descend two fieldsides to a gate into woodland. The path drops to an access road at the bottom, across which is a footbridge over Cod Beck. A steep climb slants largely right up the wooded bank to a kissing-gate at the top. With Osmotherley just in front, a hedgerowed path runs on to emerge onto a back lane. A private-looking snicket opposite leads past the Methodist chapel to emerge in novel fashion into the centre.

Opposite: Lady Chapel   Above: Scarth Wood Moor   Osmotherley

WALK 16
CARLTON MOOR

An absolutely classic stroll along a lofty moorland skyline

START *Carlton-in-Cleveland (NZ 507044; TS9 7DJ)*

DISTANCE *6¼ miles (10km)*

ORDNANCE SURVEY 1:25,000 MAP
Explorer OL26 - North York Moors West

ACCESS *Start from the village centre, roadside parking. Northallerton-Stokesley bus.*

Carlton is an attractive village strung along the road that runs south to ascend Carlton Bank onto the moors. Village pub is the Blackwell Ox, while St Botolph's church with its fine tower dates only from the late 19th century. From a bus shelter across the road from the chapel and school, drop to a double stone-slab footbridge on Alum Beck and up onto a parallel back road. Cross straight over to an access road, and quickly take a bridle-gate to the left. From another just beyond it, a hedgerowed path runs a pleasant course to a footbridge at the far end. Turn briefly left to the field corner, then resume your course along a very long sheep pasture. Through a bridle-gate at the end, drop right a few yards and once again resume your course with a fence on the left. *Ahead is distinctive, densely-wooded Whorl Hill.* Over a footbridge at the end, an enclosed path runs on to reach a path junction. The more inviting left branch runs enclosed to a bridle-gate at Faceby's village hall.

CARLTON MOOR • WALK 16

Go right on the short access road, then right along the road into Faceby alongside the Sutton Arms pub.

From this junction go left on cul-de-sac Bank Lane, and at the first chance quickly detour right on Church Lane to the church just ahead. *With its little bell-cote, St Mary Magdalene's dates largely from 1875. Opposite is a former Methodist Chapel of 1866.* Now go left along a hedgerowed grassy bridleway past the old chapel. Soon rejoining the road resume right, rising gently past the last straggling houses to end on a minor brow alongside High Farm. The continuing cart track drops gently then rises away to a choice of gates. From a bridle-gate in front, the track continues the short way up to the foot of waiting Faceby Plantation. As the

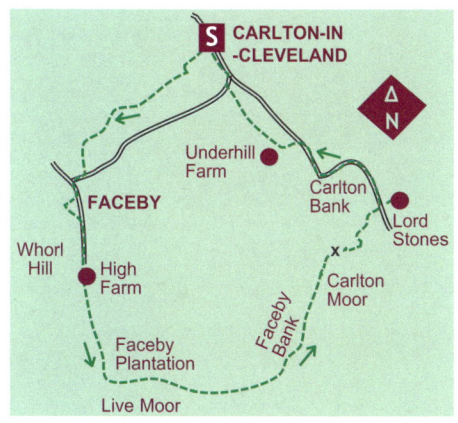

track swings left, take a path rising directly away for a short, steep climb to a bridle-gate at the wood-top. Entering dense bracken slopes, the path runs left above the trees, immediately crossing spoil heaps from former jet workings. The path runs for some time, ignoring a footpath sign for a right branch part way on. Shortly after commencing a gentle rise it finally leaves the forest fence, and slants more firmly up the slope. This excellent short climb rises to soon ease out and enter tracts of heather. It now runs the short way along to meet the Cleveland Way path in a saddle in the broad ridge dropping from Live Moor to your right.

Turn left for a super stride on a super path, surrounded for the most part by heather. *Big views look right over the deep trough of Scugdale with Bilsdale TV mast beyond, and ahead to Carlton Moor itself.* You quickly pass an 'A/F' boundary stone before a short pull above Faceby Bank onto the edge of Carlton Moor. Height is only gradually gained, the adjacent steep western scarp contrasting

WALK 16 • CARLTON MOOR

well with the heather carpet of the moor-top. *Now indiscernible to your right is the old runway of the Newcastle & Teesside (later Carlton Moor) Gliding Club. Only in the 21st century did it fold, with the eyesore buildings dismantled in 2013 to help restore the site.* The path leads unfailingly to the Ordnance Survey column and boundary stone on Carlton Moor's summit at 1338ft/408m.

Carlton Moor rises to a well-defined top perched above a steep fall to the Cleveland Plain. This is a summit on which to linger - select a heathery couch beneath the exposed top and see how many communities can be identified with the aid of the OS map. The nearest, appropriately, is Carlton, literally at your feet. Descent is swift, with the road-top on Carlton Bank already being in sight. The path keeps firmly above extensive old alum workings to drop to their right, then it winds less steeply left to drop to a kissing-gate onto a stony track. *If not visiting Lord Stones café you can cut a tiny corner by turning left here to the road.* Otherwise, cross straight over and down onto the road at Carlton Bank. From a bridle-gate opposite, a path runs briefly through trees to the Lord Stones café and car park. *This facility sits on the road summit with a popular open grassy sward alongside, where motorists can stretch their legs and effortlessly enjoy extensive views.*

For the final stage return to the road: a minor short-cut path leaves the incoming path by bearing right into dense trees the short way to a bridle-gate onto the road. Either way turn right (north), quickly swinging steeply downhill. *Impressive to your right are the scars of more alum workings beyond an extremely steep drop.* The road winds down to a cattle-grid off the moor, and continue down as far as a driveway left to Underhill Farm. Pass through the stile by a gate set back, and just a little further is a fork in front of another gate. Take the initially overgrown path right, instantly improving as it drops to a ladder-stile, with a gate just below into a rolling sheep pasture. Maintain this straight line down several fieldsides. *Look back to the aggressive front of Carlton Moor with a distinct line of alum spoil heaps at mid-height.* Ultimately you emerge at a bridle-gate onto a road at the village edge. Go briefly right on verges, then bear left on a surfaced path alongside a small green, dropping to a footbridge on Alum Beck and up onto a road end. Advance briefly on, soon forking right to a setted ford and footbridge back onto the street.

ABOVE THE LEVEN

WALK 17

Paths and tracks link contrasting villages above a shy river

START *Hutton Rudby (NZ 469063; TS15 0DL)*

DISTANCE *5¾ miles (9¼km)*

ORDNANCE SURVEY 1:25,000 MAP
Explorer OL26 - North York Moors West

ACCESS *Start from the village centre, roadside parking. Stokesley-Northallerton bus.*

Hutton Rudby is a sizeable village of great character set back from a large sloping green. There are three pubs, the Kings Head, Wheatsheaf and Bay Horse, a Post office/shop and a Methodist church of 1879 serving refreshments. Well-worn mounting steps stand outside a house with a 1745 datestone near the Kings Head, while the green features a particularly old roadsign and an old pump. From the triangular green at the foot of the main green, go right on the Swainby road just as far as The Wynd, where an enclosed firm path drops away left and into trees. It runs out to a leafy lane, but without setting foot on it, take a bridle-gate on the left just a few yards further. A broad path doubles back down the wooded slope to meet the River Leven, and follows it downstream. Around the backs of gardens it emerges at steps up onto a road at Hutton Bridge, which cross to All Saints Church. *At the back of the churchyard are the distinctive remains of an old moat.*

WALK 17 • ABOVE THE LEVEN

Across the road head away along an unsigned lane, and just short of a private bridge, take a concrete access road rising right. It soon drops back down to run to a sewage works. A path passes left to run between it and the river: emerging, faced with a belt of trees and scrub, the path splits. One bears right along the field edge, while a more commonly used one remains with the river as far as a fork, where the right branch joins the fieldside path by new tree plantings. At the very end the path runs into undergrowth in a recess, rapidly swinging right to rise up into Bank Wood. Briefly emerging at the edge, it then broadens for a short climb through the trees to a kissing-gate at the top. A good path runs left along a fieldside above the wood to a road-end at Blue Barn.

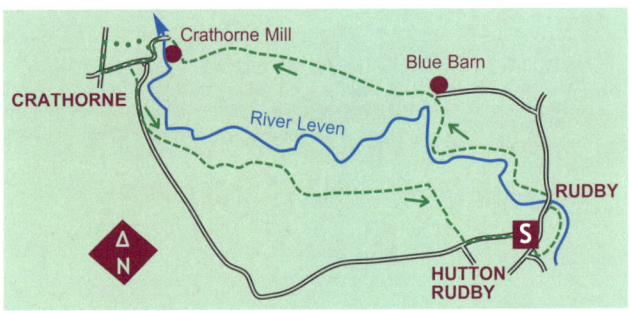

Go left in its new guise as a cart track, running outside Rudby Wood and becoming a leafy byway. Later it veers away from the wood as a hedgerowed way, then opens out to maintain a level and unerring course between arable fields. At the end, after a mile and a quarter it passes through a gate to drop more roughly down a scrubby bank to a gate at imposing red-brick Crathorne Mill. Go right on the access road past old stables, becoming surfaced to swing round to cross Crathorne Mill Bridge on the Leven. The road doubles back up a bank to emerge by Crathorne church. However there is a commonly used alternative, courtesy of the landowner. As you start going uphill from the bridge, a fieldside path runs right beneath a wood to turn a corner into a recess. Here a good path delves into trees, bridging a streamlet and heading away. It rises above the stream then winds briefly up, bearing right to run to a small gate onto the road opposite the Crathorne Arms. Turn left.

ABOVE THE LEVEN • WALK 17

Crathorne is an old estate village with much of interest. The Crathornes were Lords of the Manor into the 19th century: their Roman Catholic faith explains the presence of St Mary's church of around 1820. All seen as you pass through are the following: a tiny Post office/shop that seemingly only finally closed in 2023; an old milestone pointing to Yarm, Thirsk and London; the old school (a fine building); a Reading Room that is now a village hall; the Catholic church; the old rectory; and All Saints church. Outside of the village stands the immense Crathorne Hall, now a hotel.

Turn left on the Hutton Rudby road, and opposite the church take a kissing-gate on the right. Cross to the far left corner of a small pasture to emerge in the same way onto the road. With views soon appearing over to the Cleveland Hills, go right a few minutes as far as a gate at a small lay-by on the left. While your return is largely among arable fields, admirably broad margins are provided. Head briefly left with the hedge, quickly swinging right outside a wood. Rising gently, take a stile in the hedge to continue outside the trees. At a right-angled inner corner is a bridle-gate into the wood, and a part stepped path drops down to cross a footbridge on a streamlet, then up the other side to a bridle-gate back out. A faint path heads away along the top of a grassy bank. Entering trees ahead it improves to open out a little more, quickly swinging right into a field corner. Advance a little further above the wood to a stile into the field, where the path resumes outside the wood to quickly reach a stile/plank bridge in a hedge.

A broad path heads away on a very gentle rise across an arable field centre. At a fork on a brow, bear right to stay on the path in line with the Cleveland Hills skyline ahead. Crossing a track at a dip at a hedge-end, another very gentle rise resumes across the centre to approach a hedge. Just before it, the path bears right to run to a stile in the hedge corner. Emerging into a sheep pasture, head away with a fence, and just short of the far end take a stile in it. Cross an unkempt little corner onto a cart track, with a stile in the fence behind. A very faint path heads diagonally across a sheep pasture to a stile near the far corner in front of housing. A tiny footbridge sends a path onto a suburban street on the edge of Hutton Rudby. Go right the short way to the far end, where an enclosed path winds around to emerge onto a junction at an old North Riding roadsign. Go left on the footway to conclude.

WALK 18: RIVER WISKE

Around three very quiet villages in Wiske country

START *Appleton Wiske (NZ 390046; DL6 2AD)*

DISTANCE *5¾ miles (9¼km)*

ORDNANCE SURVEY 1:25,000 MAP
Explorer 304 - Darlington & Richmond

ACCESS *Start from the village centre, roadside parking and village hall car park. Note that the first mile by the Wiske includes a section that becomes choked with nettles in summer months (not recommended for small children at that time).*

Appleton Wiske is a pleasant village based along two streets, with Front Street boasting colourful cottages. Here are the Lord Nelson Inn, a small Post office and a particularly attractive Wesleyan Methodist Chapel of 1821. Head south on Front Street to the village edge, and immediately after the school take a kissing-gate on the left. Across a stony track an enclosed green way heads off, and remains so for some time during which you bridge a drain. The path bears right to become fully enclosed along the bank of the sluggish River Wiske. Advance along this for quite some time, as mentioned above with the prospect of summer nettles. A midway stile at a bend precedes ultimately escaping suddenly into a field. Turn right along the edge, still shadowing the stream to a corner footbridge at a stream junction. Over this and a stile just beyond,

RIVER WISKE • WALK 18

resume with the Wiske still on your right, a modest arable fieldside path forming to lead to a stile, a little beyond which is the East Coast Main Line at Wiske Railway Bridge. Through a brick-arched underpass, advance around the left side of a water treatment works ahead to join its drive. Go left on this pleasant hedgeside track all the way along to emerge opposite a nursery business on the edge of West Rounton. Turn right into the village centre.

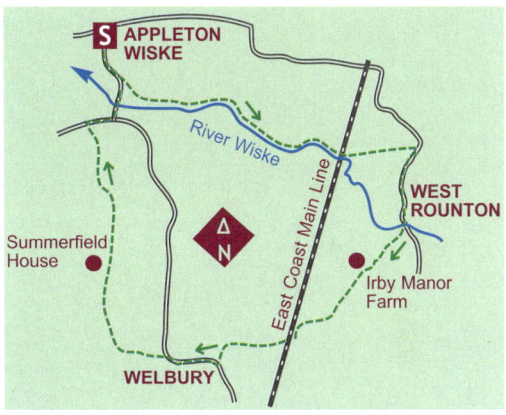

This small settlement includes St Oswald's church with twin bell-cote, Norman doorway and font, the Horseshoe Inn, a former Wesleyan Church of 1907 with working clock, and a welcome seat around a horse chestnut tree on a tiny green. At the far end drop down beneath the church to a stone-arched bridge on the Wiske. Across, take an access road rising right and running to Irby Manor Farm. Just before the buildings take a stile on the left, and bear right over the domed field to a stile/gate at a hedge-gap ahead. Head directly away past a telegraph pole to meet the railway again, where the path is deflected left by the low embankment to a small corner gate. Quickly running to a neat arched pedestrian underpass, you emerge into an arable field. A path heads directly away to soon reach a stile/gate in a hedge. Bear left around the field edge on a path running to a small corner gate, from where it runs a short, embowered course to join an access road. Go left the very short way into Welbury.

WALK 18 • RIVER WISKE

To your right is the Duke of Wellington pub, while to the left is St Leonard's church with twin bell-cote, millennium sundial and 1690 door: alongside is a fine red-brick rectory. Also on this street is a former schoolhouse of 1858. Turn right past the pub and out of the village to an open area with a seat on a bend right. Here go straight ahead along the cart track of Mankin Lane on your left, quickly becoming a super footway encased in greenery. However after only a few minutes, take an obvious gap on the right into the corner of a sloping arable field. Turning right, the true right of way veers off for Summerfield House on the skyline: being non-existent and involving trampling crops, you are instead encouraged along a splendid path with the tall hedge on your right. This preferred route avoids grief by simply continuing over the brow, all the way down to the bottom corner. It then goes left a short way with a hedge and drain to rejoin the right of way at a stile on the right.

For the record, arriving near the houses the right of way takes a fence-stile, crosses a paddock to one onto the access road. From a gate in front it crosses a messy enclosure past outbuildings to a blocked gap at the right corner. Going straight on a concrete yard left of the massive barns, it turns right along their rear and into a field corner. It heads away with a hedge on the left: when this turns off the way continues down the arable field to a hedge-stile where the alternative path comes in. Now simply head away along a very lengthy hedgeside to a stile onto a road. Go briefly right to a junction, then left over the Wiske back into the village.

At Appleton Wiske

COAST TO COAST WALK

WALK 19

Gentle fieldpaths on a famous walk's quieter stretch

START *Danby Wiske (SE 337985; DL7 0NQ)*

DISTANCE *6 miles (9½km)*

ORDNANCE SURVEY 1:25,000 MAP
Explorer 302 - Northallerton & Thirsk

ACCESS *Start from the village centre, roadside parking and car park at village hall*

One of numerous villages on the modest River Wiske that uses the stream's name as a suffix, Danby Wiske has earned a modest reputation as a staging post on the Coast to Coast Walk's long haul across the vale to Ingleby Cross, and is now a popular overnight halt. It remains the most peaceful of communities, though the sight of booted legions striding through is no longer the bizarre apparition it was. The White Swan's pub sign sports the remaining mileage to the coast, while a splendid tuck shop operates at Church Holme, with WC and camping. The attractive church has, rarely, no dedication, and incorporates work back to Norman times.

Head south out of the village past the village hall and church. Just after the last house (Glebe House), take a firm track rising gently right by a hedge. Reaching a clump of trees, leave the main track and bear left on a nicer one, soon leaving this at a gate on the right. This sends a superb enclosed pathway off on a lengthy

WALK 19 • COAST TO COAST WALK

stride through greenery, ultimately emerging on a modest brow. *The walk's summit at 187ft/57m gives views ahead to Penhill in the Yorkshire Dales.* Resume down the hedgeside, and levelling out, pass through a large gap on the right to continue on a track on the other side. At the end just ahead, the track swings right, but go very briefly left to a gap in the hedge on the right. A meagre path bears left around the field edge, rising gently and along to a tiny kink, which pass through. Resume along a fieldside and on to merge into a drive at High Brockholme. Advance along this out onto a road.

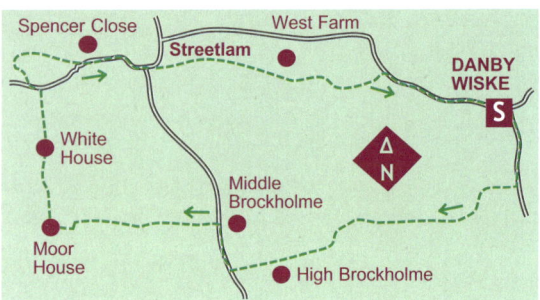

With some mown verges, go right for a few minutes until the drive to Middle Brockholme, where turn through a gateway on the left and head away with a hedge along an uninviting arable field-side. Through a gap at the end, go left around a corner and along

to the end to a footbridge on a drain. Resume directly across an arable field-path to a gate ahead, then across two further pastures with a gate midway. Now follow the fence on your left to a grouping of barns at Moor House. Just in front take a gate on your left, round the outside of the buildings to emerge by the house. Follow the drive out to an access road junction just ahead, and turn right. This runs past the attractive former White House Farm and along the hedgerowed drive to a road.

COAST TO COAST WALK • WALK 19

Whilst you could simply turn right, for variety turn left just 130 yards to Rawcar Farm drive on your right. After a couple of bends it forks: use neither, but from a gate on the right bear gently right over a field to a hedge-corner stile. Head away across a distinctive ridge and furrow pasture, with Spencer Close farm ahead. Bear right to a stile back onto the road a little short of the corner. *From here you follow the Coast to Coast Walk back to the start.* Go left for a few minutes to a junction in the hamlet of Streetlam.

Advance just a few yards towards a tiny green, where take a kissing-gate on the right. Skirt around a fence, then bear left to a corner stile into a briefly enclosed section at horse paddocks. Through gates small and large, bear left to a corner kissing-gate into trees. A good path runs along the wood edge to emerge into a rolling pasture. *Ahead are the Cleveland Hills and Black Hambleton on the edge of the North York Moors.* From here a succession of lush pastures lead on, largely in a straight line with metal kissing-gates and mostly with a hedge to your left. Along the length of this field to a kissing-gate at the end, bear slightly right to the next one, level with West Farm. Returning to the hedge at a corner you briefly follow its other side before returning to the right. Resuming initially enclosed, you bridge a drain and on a little further to meet a surfaced access road. Go left the short way out onto a road, and turn right over a brow at Park Hill to drop back down into Danby Wiske. *The first house on the right sports evidence of its past life as a North Riding Constabulary police house.*

At Danby Wiske

WALK 20 RIVER SWALE

A rare opportunity to walk the banks of the Swale

START *Ainderby Steeple (SE 333921; DL7 9PU)*

DISTANCE *5½ miles (8¾km)*

ORDNANCE SURVEY 1:25,000 MAP
Explorer 302 - Northallerton & Thirsk

ACCESS *Start from the village centre, parking by green. Bedale-Northallerton bus.*

Ainderby Steeple is a small village set around a green bearing an old milestone and split by the main road. Dating from the 14th century, St Helen's church occupies an elevated mound, though its dominant feature is its fine tower, rather than a steeple! Across the road is the Wellington Heifer pub. Leave by an enclosed cart track at the rear of the smaller green, left of the old vicarage. This runs past houses to one at the end, where it swings sharp right: instead take a gap on the left before the house, across a lawn to a stile into an arable field. A path turns right along the hedgeside for a nice stroll to a path junction at the end. *This affords views left to the Hambleton Hills and ahead to shapely Penhill in the Yorkshire Dales.* Go left on the broader grassy way dropping with a fence to a gate/stile. A good path bears right across a pasture to a corner stile, where resume left on an arable fieldside. At the

RIVER SWALE • WALK 20

corner it swings right to run along to join a farm road, Back Lane. Go left, over a cattle-grid and swinging right towards Langlands.

The true bridleway runs a largely unseen parallel course along the left side of this narrow enclosure, at the far end joining a cart track coming out from the farm. Advance on this through a gate, being briefly enclosed before opening out into a slender field. The track shadows a hedge and drain on the left, and just short of the end turns left to pass through. Heading away along a hedgeside, it turns sharp right with it at a wooded corner to continue: fading into a grassier course it runs a direct course to a bridle-gate ahead. Joining a fieldside track go left, once again swinging right around a corner to conclude as a narrower path emerging onto the farm road of Potter Lane.

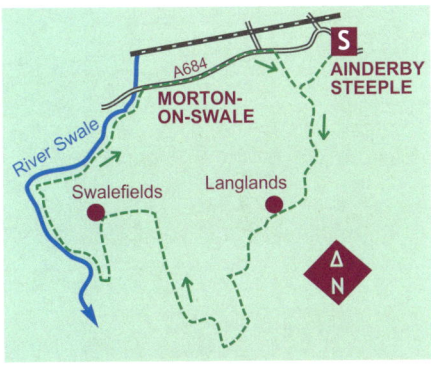

Turn right on the surfaced road, initially with a super verge. Around two sharp bends comes a longer straight section to a junction with a drive for Swalefields. Go left on its grass verged course to the farm. Level with the house, ignore a gate in front and turn left on a hedgeside track. Becoming grassier, the hedge is soon replaced by intermittent trees on your left. A little further it turns right with a fence to a gate accessing the grassy banks of the River Swale.

Turn right on a flood embankment with a decent path forming, soon gaining closer company with the serene river. This course is maintained for a good mile and a quarter through lush pasture with arable fields over the adjacent fence. A sharp bend right sees you back near the farm, and after a couple of earlier gates/stiles you reach a solitary stile where the embankment path ends. Drop left to resume through a continuing pasture, scrub-draped banks now screening the river. Narrowing then broadening between river and field boundary, the fence turns off to send your little path across a sheep pasture to a stile onto the A684 at Morton Bridge.

WALK 20 • RIVER SWALE

Cross to the footway, and without crossing the actual bridge turn right into Morton-on-Swale, remaining on this throughout the full length of the village. *Morton's features include the Old Royal George pub, a shop, a United Methodist Free Church of 1879, a Methodist Chapel of 1815 that is now the village hall, and even a butcher. Morton also lays claim to the former Ainderby station at a level-crossing just along Station Lane.* Reaching the school at the far end, take a stile on the right immediately after the last houses. A fieldside track heads away, initially outside some gardens then along to a gate/stile on a gentle brow where you rejoin your outward route. With the church tower beckoning, turn left on the good path you set out on to finish as you began.

At Ainderby Steeple

FLEETHAM & FENCOTES

WALK 21

Around a group of attractive villages off the beaten track

START *Scruton (SE 300924; DL7 0QP)*

DISTANCE *5¼ miles (8½km)*

ORDNANCE SURVEY 1:25,000 MAP
Explorer 302 - Northallerton & Thirsk

ACCESS *Start from the village centre, roadside parking. Bus from Northallerton.*

Scruton is celebrated as one of the small number of 'Thankful Villages', to which all its men returned safely from the First World War. The Coore Arms recalls owners of now demolished Scruton Hall. At the back of the village green stands St Radegund's church with a 15th century tower. Scruton's station on the Wensleydale Railway re-opened in 2015, some 60 years after closure: an old AA roadsign adorns the wall. The village hall occupies the old school of 1860. Leave by a suburban street, The Parklands, just left of the church. After it bends left, a path runs right between gardens to a stile into the vast pasture of Scruton Parklands. Bear left across the centre, aiming well to the right of a white cottage. While a stile will be found onto a road, an option is to go right between road and fence, on through an enclosure at the end, continuing to a second tiny one and bearing left to a gate onto the road.

WALK 21 • FLEETHAM & FENCOTES

Go right past Scruton Grange, and as the road bends left, advance just a few strides further to find a hedge-stile into a sheep pasture on the right. Head directly away, with a broad grassy way forming to run to a stile into a belt of trees. A tiny path crosses a streamlet to emerge via another stile on the other side. Head away with a hedge, through an old field boundary to a corner stile. Resume on an arable fieldside to a stile at the end. This sends a restrictively enclosed path away along a fieldside, causing envious eyes to be cast on the pasture itself. Mercifully escape part way on at a bridle-gate into the field. Resume to the end, with a corner stile just left of a gate. Cross to a stile ahead, and with Raisin Hall just ahead, bear left to a gate further along. Bear left again across a 'pig enclosure', passing left of a small enclosure within to find a stile alongside an old gate onto an access road, Fleetham Lane.

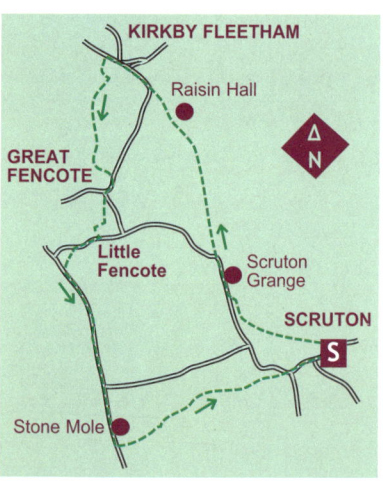

This water company road sees local use to avoid a missing stile in an untidy corner at the end of the next field: it runs left to a road alongside red-brick former Fleetham Mill. The official path takes a stile opposite and bears left on a very faint embanked way parallel with a fence just to the left. Reaching a fence enclosing trees, the current absence of a stile means striding the fence to run briefly on through a wooded corner to a stile onto a road on the edge of Kirkby Fleetham. However joined, go right to the centre. *This very pleasant village is set around an extensive green, and features the Black Horse Inn with a quoits pitch. St Mary's church stands almost a mile distant alongside Kirby Fleetham Hall.*

Advance to a staggered crossroads at the end, and keep left past the school just as far as the pub. Turn down the side of its car park to a stile in the bottom corner, and head away with a hedge.

FLEETHAM & FENCOTES • WALK 21

Part way up a slight rise, take a near-hidden stile on the left, and alongside a brick-built shed, head away to an old hedge just ahead. *Distinctive grassy earthworks a little further ahead mark the site of Kirkby Fleetham Castle, an early 14th century hunting lodge.*

Go right with the fading hedge, and outside a small wood to a grassy bridge and gate. Continue away with a fence on your left, through two pastures linked by a stile. From a gate at the end of the second, with Anna Garth Farm ahead, bear right outside its confines to join a track. Go left through a gate into the yard, then take a gate on the right to run past a modern barn to another gate. Now bear left across a field to a hedge-stile in front of houses, and out via a tiny gate onto a tiny green in Great Fencote.

This small village features a triangular green to the left with a derelict red-brick chapel. Go briefly right to a junction by St Andrew's church and an old North Riding roadsign, and go left. Very quickly go right on an old section of road, ending at a gate into an arable field. A headland path goes left, around an inner then an outer corner then along to a small gate onto a road in the hamlet of Little Fencote. Go right with a decent verge just as far as the de-restriction sign. From a stile on the left after a farm, a road junction can be cut by advancing a few yards then following a straight path between crops to an awkward stile back onto a road.

Go left for almost a mile, passing a Scruton junction. Beyond this, after the house at Stone Mole Farm, a bridle-gate on the left sends a hedgeside path gently down an arable fieldside. When the hedge turns off, a better path continues down the centre between crops. Entering a belt of trees it becomes a cart track, emerging as a firmer track to run to a cluster of barns. Passing to their left, ignore the track's right turn and keep on a broad grassy way a little further to an access road. Just five yards to the right, locate an arrow-like path heading away across the arable field to a gate at the bottom. Advance a short way to a gate on the left onto a road on the village edge, and go right to finish.

At Great Fencote

WALK 22
BOLTON-ON-SWALE

Easy strolling around a variety of interesting locations

START *Scorton (SE 242996; DL10 6AB)*

DISTANCE *6¼ miles (10km)*

ORDNANCE SURVEY 1:25,000 MAP
Explorer 304 - Darlington & Richmond

ACCESS *Start from Scorton Lakes South car park, on B6271 ¾ miles south-west of village. Northallerton-Richmond bus.*

The area south and west of Scorton was extensively quarried for sand and gravel, and since 2008 has been subject to an ongoing transformation into a now extensive nature reserve landscape. Several lakes and numerous walking routes have been created, indeed the start point overlooks Swaleside Water. By information panels a bridle-gate sends an enclosed path east parallel with the road, maintaining this course to meet Back Lane as it leaves the road. Cross to a bridle-gate sending a path down to another one on the edge of Scorton Water. Take the path running right outside its boundary fence, at the end swinging left to run above the far side of the lake. At the end the path swings right to rise briefly to a bridle-gate onto the enclosed cart track of Flat Lane. Go left for a pleasant stroll, later becoming concrete to emerge back onto the B6271 at Bolton-on-Swale. Cross to the footway and go very briefly right to the preserved village pump, then fork left to the church.

BOLTON-ON-SWALE • WALK 22

This hamlet is known far outside its bounds for its churchyard memorial to Henry Jenkins, reputedly born in 1500, and passing on 169 years later. He could recall taking a cart-load of arrows to Flodden Field in Northumberland in 1513, and also visiting the abbot at Fountains. In true English fashion, until recently an inn at Kirkby Malzeard, near Masham, recalled Henry's achievement by name. St Mary's 14th century church has a hoary 16th century tower and self-service refreshments, with a donations box.

From the church go very briefly left along the road, and at a kissing-gate bear left across a lush pasture, loosely accompanying Bolton Beck. From a kissing-gate the path traces an arable field edge with little sign of the stream. Through another bridle-gate, part way along the next field take an easily missed little bridge to resume on the other bank. Quickly emerging from an arable field, a pleasant pasture leads to a bridle-gate onto Laylands farm drive. From one opposite, bear right to a gate behind it for the path to run an enclosed course with the still hidden stream. You emerge at the end alongside a road bridge near Ellerton Hill.

Turn left for a full mile, during which time some good verges prove useful, passing extensive Plantation Farm and on between Fatten Hill and Hodber Hill Plantations. On reaching a staggered crossroads, keep left as far as a sharp bend right at Ellerton Gate. Here advance straight on into an arable field corner, your bridle-way tracing the right edge to rapidly become encased in greenery.

WALK 22 • BOLTON-ON-SWALE

This continues for some time before gradually re-emerging into the fieldside for a long steady rise onto another quiet back road. Go left for a short while, then take the drive right to Feather Hill Farm.

Go straight ahead through a gate into a concrete yard, then turn left between house and modern barns for the concrete track to end just beyond the buildings. From the left-hand of two gates in front, an enclosed cart track heads directly away on a pleasant course, which swings right and improves further before ending at a gate into an arable field corner. A broad grassy headland runs left to a gate at the end. A short path bridges Scorton Beck to arrive at a corner outside gardens on the edge of Scorton. Go left on a path to a gate into the grounds of the Coach House: the short drive runs out past red-brick Manor House to emerge into the centre.

This attractive village sits around a vast green which doubles as an enormous roundabout. It has a Post office/shop, the Farmers Arms and Heifer pubs, and a Methodist Church of 1909. Prominent at the north-east corner of the green is the distinguished frontage of a grammar school founded around 1760 but now converted to residential use. Over the road was the Hospital of St John of God: with a Roman Catholic chapel of 1823, it cared for the elderly for over 100 years until the turn of this century.

Leave at the south-west corner of the green to your left, and quickly take a bridle-gate on the right after the last houses. A grassy path strikes diagonally away across this pasture to one in a tall hedge ahead. Joining an enclosed bridleway, go briefly left to a gate into more open surrounds, and bear right on the broader way running towards Tancred Grange Farm. Faced with a gate the path instead kinks right, and runs an enclosed course with Grange Lake to your right. The path swings left to merge into the farmyard access road, which leads out onto the B6271. Cross to re-enter the car park.

Henry Jenkins Memorial, Bolton

HARTFORTH & WHASHTON

WALK 23

Much interest in and around the valley of Hartforth Beck

START *Gilling West (NZ 182050; DL10 5JG)*

DISTANCE *6 miles (9½km)*

ORDNANCE SURVEY 1:25,000 MAP
Explorer 304 - Darlington & Richmond

ACCESS *Start from the village centre on B6274, parking near church entrance. Bus from Richmond, Barnard Castle, Darlington.*

Gilling West is a very attractive street village, with a green at its northern end. St Agatha's church dates from the 11th century, while the White Swan was a coaching inn. Just along the street is the Angel Inn, also a blacksmith, a florist and a former school of 1847. From the northern end of Gilling Bridge on Gilling Beck, advance just a few strides to a kissing-gate on the left. An enclosed path heads out of the village, and on emerging into a field, it runs on to cross an access road. From a bridle-gate behind, commence a super course through numerous pastures. Ultimately entering an arable field, the path surmounts a modest brow and runs arrow-like to the far end to enter the hamlet of Hartforth.

Advance along the short access road to a sharp bend right, then keep on a short way to go left beyond the buildings at Home Farm. This grassy bridleway of historic Jagger Lane drops down to a splendid three-arched bridge on Hartforth Beck. *Back to your left*

WALK 23 • HARTFORTH & WHASHTON

is the imposing and award-winning 21st century replacement for Home Farm, while viewed upstream is Hartforth Hall. This fine country house of 1744 was until very recently a hotel. Across the bridge turn sharp right on a path across the park-like field centre. A similar path following the beck upstream is not the right of way. With good views of the hall, you join a firm access track at the far end. Cross the footbridge alongside a ford, and leave the track by going left on a broad path tracing the beck. At a recess further along, the path bears left onto an access road, going left towards a secluded house at Hartforth Mill. The path quickly leaves the drive to run upstream to a footbridge, across which it runs briefly through trees. Emerging, remain on the path upstream with a fence, a super stroll that traces it all the way along its winding course to reach a minor road at single-arched Whashton Bridge.

Immediately before the road take a stile on the left, and ascend the fieldside to merge with a hedge further to the right. Continue up to a stile/gate just short of a corner, and head away on an initially faint path. Broadening into a track rising up the arable field, it eases out towards the top and bears right to a corner gate back onto the road. Without joining it take a stile in the hedge on your left, and ascend a field to one above, just left of a gate. An enclosed path rises to a stile, to then rise past a cottage and up its short drive into Whashton. *This small linear village features a long slender green with a quoits pitch, while on your right is the former Hack & Spade pub, now a guesthouse.*

HARTFORTH & WHASHTON • WALK 23

Go left on the road out, dropping towards its demise at Whashton Hag. Just before the dip, a gate on the left sends a wallside path away, bearing right at the end to a gate ahead. Rising into trees outside Hartforth Wood, it runs grandly on to drop at the end to a ford with stepping-stones on wooded Smelt Mill Beck. *Low ruins on the left are the scant remains of a lead mining site.* Steeply up the other side, head away on an unkempt track, improving towards the end to meet a firmer one (Jagger Lane again). Double back right up its gentle wallside course, passing an old quarry as it levels out.

Through a cattle-grid/gate in front it continues up the wallside. As the wall turn sharp left, rise just a little further to a gate in the continuing fence, and a grassy way heads off beneath gorse and trees above the wall. At a gate at the end into a sloping pasture, the path fades as you unfailingly shadow the wall. At the end bear right on a path outside The Ashes (a wood) up to a gate. Resume on a final fieldside to a gate into Gillingwood Hall's farming environs. A grassy way drops below barns to a gate into the yard, leaving by the access road. *Up to the right is a pair of follies, created by the Whartons who occupied the original house destroyed by fire in 1750.*

Further on, your way turns sharp left to drop away. *Easiest option is to remain on this onto Waters Lane, going right to finish.* Leave at an early wall-gap on the right, and a thin path drops slightly away across an arable field. At the far side drop left with a fence beneath a wooded bank, soon reaching a gap with a stile just behind. Drop left down a nicer pasture, bearing left to a grassy bridge on a dyke. Bear right to a stile ahead, and through unkempt surrounds with a wildfowl pond to your right. Soon emerging at the base of a sloping field on your left, cross to a stile a short way up the facing hedge. From another one ahead, bear left over the brow to reveal the village ahead. Drop to a corner gate, then along a hedgeside as far as a slim stile by an outbuilding on the right. This sends an enclosed path between gardens to emerge back onto the street. Go left to finish past an old milestone pointing to Richmond and Lucy Cross.

WALK 24: KIRBY HILL & DALTON

Plentiful scenery and history on interesting paths linking a series of characterful hillside villages

START *Ravensworth (NZ 140078; DL11 7ET)*

DISTANCE *6¼ miles (10km)*

ORDNANCE SURVEY 1:25,000 MAP
Explorer 304 - Darlington & Richmond

ACCESS *Start from the village centre, roadside parking. Richmond-Barnard Castle bus.*

The very attractive village of Ravensworth is spread around the edges of extensive greens, with the Bay Horse pub at the centre and a small Methodist church nearby. On the edge of the village stand the scattered remains of Ravensworth Castle, a 14th century fortified manor house of the Fitzhughs. Facing the pub, leave by the side road going left across a green to quickly leave the houses alongside the school. The castle is best seen from this vicinity, across a wildlife pond. As the road quickly bends sharp right, advance straight on over a cattle-grid on Larklands Farm drive.

Before long take a stile on the left, over stepping-stones on a streamlet. Slant away up the field, crossing a bank and ditch to a stile above. Head away with a wallside path, rising then running on to a wall-stile at the end. An initially thin path ascends the steep, colourful Saltern Bank, passing a memorial stone and curving more clearly left to a wall-stile at the top. From this old churchgoers' path pause to look back over the village, with the castle inevitably prominent. A little path bears right up a small enclosure to a stile onto the road at Kirby Hill, emerging between the church and the Shoulder of Mutton pub. *Historically Kirby-on-the-Hill, this tiny village is based around a square green dominated by the medieval church of St Peter & St Felix with its very solid tower. Alongside is the old grammar school originally founded in 1556 (extended in 1706), while across the green are the former Dakin's Almshouses (originally St John the Baptist's Hospital) founded in 1754.*

Turn right on the road out, but soon leave by an enclosed cart track on the left. Through a gate it passes a fine double limekiln, and from a gate just behind, slants right up a field centre. Through a facing gate just short of the top corner, the splendid green way of

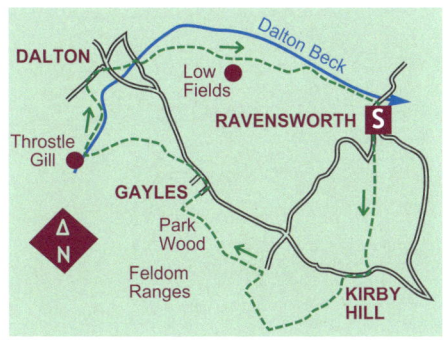

Hergill Lane rises very steadily to meet a firmer access road at the top. *To the left and ahead is the MOD's Feldom Ranges.* Turn right for a good stride, soon dropping past a lone house to a sharp right turn. Dropping more firmly, leave by a stile/gate set back on the left before reaching Quarry House. A grassy track heads away, maintaining a largely level course through the gorse- and bracken-draped environs of Gayles Quarry. *Closed as long ago as 1895, at time of research there was a controversial application to re-open.*

Emerging, the way fades as you advance on with a fence to your right. Crossing a streamlet below a small ravine, cross to a ladder-stile in the wall ahead into Park Wood. Advance a few strides to join a clearer path dropping right, and pleasantly along to a stile out of the trees. A splendid green way slants down across a sloping pasture to a fence, then dropping briefly to a gate where fence and wall meet. Head away with a fence on your left to a gate onto the access road of Gayles Hall, to your left. Turn down this

WALK 24 • KIRBY HILL & DALTON

into Gayles. *This tiny village features numerous attractive dwellings, the first house on your right being the hugely attractive Manor House dating from the late 17th century.* At the through road go left to the next junction, noting the former Bay Horse pub.

Keep straight on to the de-restriction sign, just 100 yards after which take a stile on the left. Ascend the fieldside to a gate above, just after which bear right to a stile and plank bridge at a lone tree. Continue the slant across a larger field to a stile/gate in the far corner. A path crosses an arable field, rising very gently to meet a firm track at the end. Through a gate in front, leave by dropping right past a tiny pond to a footbridge over lively Dalton Beck, with a house at Throstle Gill to the left. Turn downstream to a small gate into the beck's wooded environs, and a good path heads away. After an early sidestream you are briefly deflected away by a rocky little gorge, but the path continues close by the beck through some charming surrounds to reach the former Dalton Mill over a sidestream bridge. In the yard turn sharp left up the drive to join a road on the edge of Dalton. Turn right the short way down to the centre. *The walk's final village is based around the island church of St James, with small greens at a road junction with the former Travellers Rest pub close by.*

Kirby Hill church

*Opposite:
Dalton Beck at
Ravensworth*

KIRBY HILL & DALTON • WALK 24

Leave by turning right from the junction, and just 25 yards after the bus shelter a stile sends a short, enclosed path left between gardens to a stile into a sheep pasture. Cross to the far end, bearing right to a corner gate onto Low Lane. Go right over Low Bridge on Dalton Beck, then turn left into a concrete farmyard at Gayles Fields. Pass between beck and barns to a gate out into a field at the end. Bear right of a house, and go briefly right to a stile in the facing hedge. A firm path heads away across a large, arable field, quickly bearing right on an arrow-like course to arrive at a ramshackle stile at the far end. Resume across another arable field, shadowing a detached hedge (with the farm at Low Fields to the right) which points you to a gate in the wall ahead.

Cross a smaller such field to a colourful knoll, which a small path surmounts. Down the other side to a small gate, bear left across the field to a grassy embankment. Behind it is a ford (not used) on Dalton Beck. Turn right on an embankment path that shadows the stream along to a stile into a lush pasture. The final stage enjoys a delectable streamside stroll to a gate by a stone-arched bridge (again, not used) at the far end. A track heads away past new housing, soon swinging right out onto the road back into the village. Go right the short way back into the centre.

WALK 25 — STANWICK FORT

The earthen ramparts of an Iron Age fort are central feature of a cluster of interesting villages and hamlets

START Aldbrough St John (NZ 202114; DL11 7SZ)

DISTANCE 6¼ miles (10km)

ORDNANCE SURVEY 1:25,000 MAP
Explorer 304 - Darlington & Richmond

ACCESS *Start from the village centre, roadside parking and by village hall. Richmond-Darlington bus.*

Aldbrough St John is an elegant village set back from a pair of greens, with extensive Low Green overlooked by Aldbrough Hall. Aldbrough Beck flows through the centre, and is crossed by a fine packhorse bridge (see back cover) on a major medieval route. The smaller High Green alongside has a quoits pitch, and is overlooked by the Stanwick Arms and a former school. Alongside the village hall are a former Wesleyan Methodist Chapel and a pinfold, while St Paul's little church features a bell-turret. An annual summer festival of local renown is known simply as The Feast. The Roman road Dere Street runs less than a mile to the east, now the B6275.

From High Green outside the pub, cross to the near-hidden packhorse bridge opposite. Onto a small green, go right just yards to distinctive gateposts. Immediately through, take a gate on the right and head along the field close by the beck. At the tapering end cross a footbridge on inflowing Mary Wild Beck by a ford, and through a gate into a large, rolling pasture. Rise steadily left on a tractor track, crossing the nearby fence on your left at a stile/gate, and resuming with the fence. When it bends gently right to a corner, continue straight up a faint path to a stile/gate ahead. Advancing to a brow just ahead, bear gently right down towards a fence where it meets a road. *Note the first sighting of the Stanwick Fortifications across to the left, of which more shortly.*

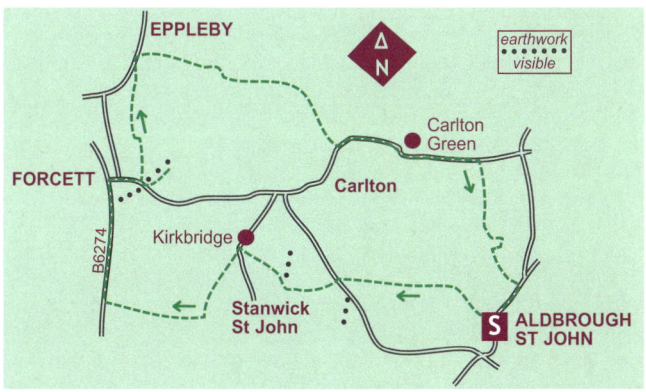

From a stile onto the road, go 40 yards left to one opposite, and head away along a narrow strip by Mary Wild Beck. Through a gate at the end, Stanwick church appears ahead. Advance on a path with the clear stream, crossing it towards the end to a stile up onto a road at Kirkbridge. *Impressive Kirkbridge House on your right dates from the 17th century.* While the onward route is through a bridle-gate opposite, first cross Kirk Bridge to visit the church of St John the Baptist in a charming setting. *Its solid tower dates from the 13th century, while inside are a 9th century Viking cross and a splendid effigy of Sir Hugh Smithson and his wife.*

Back at the bridle-gate, a grassy path rises away through the pasture of the Tofts. *To your right a hexagonal deer shelter stands on the site of an 18th century ice-house, at what was the centre of the Iron Age site. Stanwick Fortifications are a remarkable earthwork of the Brigantes, whose settlement of around 700 acres was defended by a network of banks and ditches. This powerful*

WALK 25 • STANWICK FORT

tribe controlled much of Northern England (Brigantia) prior to and during the Roman invasion that began in the mid-1st century. Built by Venutius shortly after the invasion, his wife Cartimandua replaced him as leader, and while she accepted Roman control, he later fought against both her and the invaders. Whilst the balance of power fluctuated, ultimately Roman supremacy prevailed.

A gate in the top corner sends a short-lived enclosed way along between a wall and a wood into a field corner. Go left on a track to a junction on a gentle brow. Turn right, a better track rising ever gently along a crest between arable fields, then running on as a path to shadow Hillhouse Plantation to a road junction. Turn right on the B6274 down into the hamlet of Forcett. *Approaching it, a distinct section of earthwork stands to your right. On the left is St Cuthbert's church with a 13th century tower, just past which are early 18th century gates and lodges at the entrance to Forcett Hall.*

At the junction turn right the few yards to another, then right again at an old North Riding roadsign. Immediately at the last house is your onward route, but first advance 50 yards to an information panel. A kissing-gate on the left puts you up onto the embankment for a short stroll along a fine section of the fortifications. Although a path continues further, early wooden steps drop down into the deep ditch to double back along it to the road. Just to the right take a driveway curving up towards buildings. *The true path takes an old stile and crosses a paddock to a blocked one back onto the drive.* On your right is a stile into an equestrian paddock, where bear left to a corner stile. Head away through unkempt grassland

with a hedge on your left, and at the end a stile puts you into an arable field. Go briefly left to the corner, then right with the hedge to the far end. A stile puts you onto a level track. *This is the course of the Forcett Railway that opened in 1867 and ran some 8 miles from the Darlington-Barnard Castle line near Piercebridge to serve quarries near the hamlet.* From a stile opposite, head away to cross a reedy area to a plank bridge on Forcett Beck. Now cross a sheep pasture to a corner gate onto a driveway accessing the road through Eppleby. Go right to the centre. *Here are extensive greens with houses set back, a shop/tearoom and the Cross Keys pub.*

Turn right to the far end of the first green, and a cart track heads away to sewage works. An onward path runs outside its grounds to a wicket-gate back onto the old railway. Across, a broad, arable fieldside path heads away with Aldbrough Beck largely hidden on your right. This happy state continues through long fields to emerge via a hedge-gap onto a back road at Oak Wood. Go left for a long half-mile, passing Carlton Green. At a minor kink 200 yards after a drive right to Carlton Park Farm, a fence-gap on the right sends a hedgeside path down an arable field. At the bottom corner, resume in the next field around a double recess. A short way further you reach a stile at a wall-end, where leave the field and head away alongside horse paddocks. Initially enclosed, it opens out to run to a corner stile sending a short-lived path between gardens out onto the road on the village edge. Turn right to finish.

Opposite:
In Stanwick church

Aldbrough St John

INDEX • *Walk number refers*

Ainderby Steeple	20
Aldbrough St John	25
Appleton Wiske	18
Bedale	7
Boltby	12
Bolton-on-Swale	22
Borrowby	13
Braithwaite Hall	4
Caldbergh	4
Carlton-in-Cleveland	16
Carlton Moor	16
Castle Steads	4
Cod Beck	11
Constable Burton	6
Cover, River	4,5
Cover Bridge	5
Crakehall	7
Crathorne	17
Dalton	24
Danby Wiske	19
Easby Abbey	1
East Witton	5
Ellingstring	5
Eppleby	25
Faceby	16
Felixkirk	12
Finghall	4
Forcett	25
Gayles	24
Gilling West	23
Great Fencote	21
Harmby	3
Hartforth	23
Hudswell	2
Hudswell Woods	2
Hutton Rudby	17
Jervaulx Abbey	5
Kirby Hill	24
Kirby Knowle	12
Kirkby Fleetham	21
Knayton	13
Leven, River	17
Leyburn	3
Little Fencote	21
Lord Stones	16
Maunby	10
Middleham	4
Middleham Low Moor	4
Morton-on-Swale	20
Nether Silton	14
Nosterfield	8
Osmotherley	15
Over Silton	14
Pickhill	10
Ravensworth	24
Richmond	1,2
Scarth Wood Moor	15
Scorton	22
Scruton	21
Sinderby	10
Snape	9
South Kilvington	11
Sowerby	11
Stanwick Fort	25
Stanwick St John	25
Streetlam	19
Swale, River	1,2,10,20
Thimbleby	14
Thirsk	11
Thornborough	8
Thornborough Henges	8
Thornton Steward	6
Thornton Steward Res	6
Ure, River	3,5
Welbury	18
Well	9
Wensley	3
Wensleydale Rly	3,6,7
West Rounton	18
Whashton	23
Wiske, River	18